# DESTINED FOR SALVATION

## Study Book

**Also by Kalen Fristad:**

*DESTINED FOR SALVATION:*
*God's Promise to Save Everyone*
170 pages

To invite Rev. Fristad to speak to your church or group, or order copies of this book ($5.95; ten or more, $5.45), or his other book ($11.95; ten or more, $10.95), contact Destined For Salvation Ministries: 1403 W. 2$^{nd}$ St. N., Newton, Iowa 50208, 641-787-9040, www.universalistchristians.org.

This Study Book is for adults and youth. While it is designed to be used by itself with no supplemental material, it would be helpful for the leader to use Rev. Fristad's other book as an additional resource.

# DESTINED FOR SALVATION

## God's Promise to Save Everyone

## Study Book

# Kalen Fristad

ISBN:  0-9729625-1-4

First Printing June - 2003

Scripture quotations, unless otherwise noted, are from the New
Revised Standard Version of the Bible, copyrighted in 1989 by the
Division of Christian Education of the National Council
of the Churches of Christ in the U.S.A.

Photo of Kalen Fristad on back cover by John Lee Photography.

Cover Photography Copyright © 1997 by Morris Press

Printed in the United States by Morris Publishing
3212 East Highway 30 • Kearney, NE  68847
1-800-650-7888

# CONTENTS

# PREFACE

I have written this book to let the world in on a secret that the Church has kept away from most people for the last 1,400 years. This is the secret: *God will eventually save everyone.* This truth, supported by the Bible, was widely accepted by early Christians for over 500 years. The belief in universal salvation was threatening to some Church leaders and the teaching was banished in the sixth century. In the eighteenth century, Christians once again began to affirm Universalism. Since then, many theologians, church leaders and millions of Christians have espoused it. God promises to save everyone, so there is hope for us all.

The hope of universal salvation stands in bold contrast to what many people claim to be good news. That is, God succeeds in saving those who have the good sense to become converted before death, but for the others, God throws them into hell and tosses away the key.

Thoughtful people are justified in rebelling against a God who would do such a thing. They seem to instinctively know that God is not condemning, but loving and saving. They consider the perception of the God of eternal damnation, as commonly taught by most Christian churches, to be incredibly bad news. The belief that God will not or cannot save everyone, and even imposes and enforces everlasting punishment, turns many people against God. That often results in spiritual tragedies, such as atheism, meaninglessness, meanness, and Satanism.

I too rebel against the teaching of a God of eternal damnation. Two of the most basic tenets of my faith are that God is unconditionally loving and is all-powerful. It is because of those two foundational beliefs and the specific support of universalism in the Bible that I am compelled to believe in it. A God who, out of love, desperately wants to save everyone but is unable to accomplish it, is not much of a God. By the same token, a God who is quite capable of saving everyone but callously chooses to not do so is not much of a God. But the all-powerful and all-loving God as presented in the Scriptures, and in whom I believe, has enough love and power to save all of humankind.

This book is for those who are not content with the common teachings regarding God and everlasting punishment in hell, for those who are seeking more profound spiritual truth, and for those who are in outright rebellion against the Church, and even against God. I invite you to join me in exploring the issue of universalism and why it is so important for the people of today and will be for those in the generations to come.

# Lesson One

# INTRODUCTION

I was in seminary when Leslie Weatherhead (mid-twentieth century Church leader and pastor of City Temple, London) sparked my interest in the subject of universal salvation. In his book, *When the Lamp Flickers*, Weatherhead said Jesus taught that God would eventually save everyone. Weatherhead's premise held such a ring of truth and was so compelling that it set me off on a twenty-year journey of research, to learn everything I could about Universalism and why it is so important.

I learned that most people have never heard of the idea that God will eventually save everyone. Instead, they have been told throughout their lives that some people go to heaven and others go to hell. Without giving it much thought, most of them accept that conclusion.

When I tell people about universal salvation, their response is often quite favorable even though it is a new idea to most of them. A few people have given it much thought and have already rejected the idea of eternal damnation. They commonly respond with an enthusiastic expression of deep appreciation that someone finally articulated to them what they have always believed.

Universalism was a widely held belief during the early Church, has been espoused through the centuries by numerous theologians, and many people have always been receptive to it. I began to wonder why today so few people have heard that Universalism is grounded in biblical validity. And why is it that those who have come to believe in universal salvation through their own study or reasoning rarely speak up to let others know what they believe?

Speaking from my own personal experience as a minister, I have found that by making the slightest mention of it, I run the risk of experiencing judgment and wrath. Some people get quite upset and confrontational over the idea that God will eventually save everyone. They seem very threatened by it; tell me how wrong they think I am, and may even suggest that they believe I am so misguided I am in serious jeopardy of spending eternity in hell. No one wants to hear those damning words. I've learned over the years not to feel devastated by such attacks. Many people, however, choose to avoid the need to endure such severe criticism. As a result, most people who believe in universal salvation have been intimidated into silence.

Experiencing attacks from those who disagree with us shouldn't surprise us. After all, Jesus was also often severely criticized by those who saw things differently from him. But Jesus was not intimidated. He spoke freely of God's love, mercy, grace and forgiveness, and God's desire to save all people. Some self-righteous religious leaders (the scribes and Pharisees) believed Jesus was compromising the faith and leading people astray by portraying God as too loving and forgiving. After all, Jesus claimed that even notorious sinners such as prostitutes and tax collectors would be saved.

Jesus, in an encounter with the chief priests and the elders of the people who were not receptive to John the Baptist or himself, said, "Truly I tell you, the tax collectors and the prostitutes are going into the kingdom of God ahead of you" (Matthew 21:31). On another occasion, while Jesus "sat at dinner in the house, many tax collectors and sinners came and were sitting with him and his disciples. When the Pharisees saw this, they questioned his disciples, 'Why does your teacher eat with tax collectors and sinners?'" (Matthew 9:10-11).

The self-righteous begrudged God's generosity, mercy and forgiveness. In effect, they were saying, "How dare you accept the likes of those people, Jesus! We are much better than they. We have worked decades in faithful service to God, but you accept them as though they were just as good as us. It's not right! It's not fair! It's not just!"

In spite of what the scribes, Pharisees and others said, Jesus continued to preach and teach of God's limitless love, mercy, grace and forgiveness; illustrated in the parable of the Prodigal Son, according to Luke 15:11-32:

> [11]Then Jesus said, "There was a man who had two sons. [12]The younger of them said to his father, 'Father, give me the share of the property that will belong to me.' So he divided his property between them. [13]A few days later the younger son gathered all he had and traveled to a distant country, and there he squandered his property in dissolute living. [14]When he had spent everything, a severe famine took place throughout that country, and he began to be in need. [15]So he went and hired himself out to one of the citizens of that country, who sent him to his fields to feed the pigs. [16]He would gladly have filled himself with the pods that the pigs were eating; and no one gave him anything. [17]But when he came to himself he said, 'How many of my father's hired hands have bread enough to spare, but here I am dying of hunger! [18]I will get up and go to my father, and I will say to him, "Father, I have sinned against heaven and before you; [19]I am no longer worthy to be called your son; treat me like one of your hired hands."' [20]So he set off and went to his father. But while he was still far off, his father saw him and was filled with compassion; he ran and put his arms around him and kissed him. [21]Then the son said to him, 'Father, I have sinned against heaven and before you; I

am no longer worthy to be called your son.' [22]But the father said to his slaves, 'Quickly, bring out a robe—the best one—and put it on him; put a ring on his finger and sandals on his feet. [23]And get the fatted calf and kill it, and let us eat and celebrate; [24]for this son of mine was dead and is alive again; he was lost and is found!' And they began to celebrate.

[25]Now the elder son was in the field; and when he came and approached the house, he heard music and dancing. [26]He called one of the slaves and asked what was going on. [27]He replied, 'Your brother has come, and your father has killed the fatted calf, because he has got him back safe and sound.' [28]Then he became angry and refused to go in. His father came out and began to plead with him. [29]But he answered his father, 'Listen! For all these years I have been working like a slave for you, and I have never disobeyed your command; yet you have never given me even a young goat so that I might celebrate with my friends. [30]But when this son of yours came back, who has devoured your property with prostitutes, you killed the fatted calf for him!' [31]Then the father said to him, 'Son, you are always with me, and all that is mine is yours. [32]But we had to celebrate and rejoice, because this brother of yours was dead and has come to life; he was lost and has been found.'"

This parable captures perfectly the letter as well as the spirit of Jesus' teachings. What Jesus taught regarding unconditional love and acceptance of sinners is illustrated by the father accepting with open arms his wayward son. In the parable, the father represents God. This Scripture gives us confidence that God will eventually welcome into heaven not only those who remain faithful throughout their lives, as did the older son, but those who go astray as well.

The self-righteous religious leaders of Jesus' day could not accept much of what Jesus taught, and his close association with obvious sinners especially offended them. In an attempt to preserve the faith, as they understood it, they were highly critical of Jesus. That led to his crucifixion.

That same confrontation has continued ever since. Well-meaning people who see themselves as preservers of the true faith commonly criticize those who suggest that God will eventually save everyone. As a result, many people are intimidated into silence, and some even turn away from the Christian faith because they cannot accept the concept of a God of eternal damnation.

It has become very clear to me that it is true, and biblical, that God will eventually save everyone. We, therefore, must stand up for this great truth and speak out about it, even though it may subject us to the criticism of others.

In an attempt to do justice to this complex issue, we will consider it from various perspectives; beginning with what the Bible has to say.

STUDY/DISCUSSION QUESTIONS:
1. What have you been taught about heaven and hell and people's eternal destiny?
2. Have you heard that there is a biblical basis for concluding that God will eventually save everyone?
3. Can you understand how some people could be intimidated into silence regarding their beliefs on universalism?
4. Preserving the faith is important, but how might we not be like the Pharisees and thus, avoid crucifying those who may, in fact, be calling us to the true faith?
5. What if his critics had intimidated Jesus?
6. What does the welcome the Prodigal Son received from his father suggest to you regarding the prospect of God eventually saving everyone?

Lesson Two

# DARE TO POSSESS THE TRUTH

## What Does The Bible Say Regarding Universal Salvation?

Have you ever noticed that the Bible sometimes seems to speak with more than one voice on a particular topic? One example of this is with regard to God's universal grace. Some passages suggest that conversion must take place in this life because following death, one goes either to heaven or hell for eternity. Other passages indicate that God will eventually save everyone, including those initially condemned to hell. To discern the truth, we will need to consider all relevant passages on both sides of this issue, as well as some general themes in the Bible.

### Scripture That Raises Questions
### About Universal Salvation
**1. Matthew 13:24-30, 36-43**

Jesus told a parable of a man who sowed good seed in his field, but an enemy sowed weeds among the man's wheat. Rather than pulling the weeds and risking uprooting the wheat at the same time, the man told his slaves, "[30]Let both of them grow together until the harvest; and at harvest time I will tell the reapers, Collect the weeds first and bind them in bundles to be burned, but gather the wheat into my barn." Jesus explained to his disciples that "[38]the weeds are the children of the evil one, [39]and the enemy who sowed them is the devil; the harvest is the end of the age, and the reapers are angels. [40]Just as the weeds are collected and burned up with fire, so will it be at the end of the age." This passage makes it very clear that hell is terrible and that it will be experienced by the unsaved following death. It does not indicate that hell is without end.

**2. Matthew 25:1-13**

Jesus said that the kingdom of heaven will be like ten bridesmaids who took their lamps to meet the bridegroom. Five of them were wise and brought extra oil for their lamps, but the others foolishly neglected to do so. The bridegroom was so long in arriving that the lamps of the foolish bridesmaids began to run out of oil. While they were gone to buy more oil, "[10]the bridegroom came, and those who were ready went with him into the wedding banquet; and the door was shut. [11]Later the other bridesmaids came also, saying, 'Lord, lord, open to us.' [12]But he replied, 'Truly I tell you, I do not know you.' [13]Keep awake therefore, for you know neither the day nor the hour."

The bridegroom in this case represents Christ, the wedding banquet is heaven and the shutting of the door is death. It is tragic to be left out, so everyone is well advised to be ready to meet God at any time. Again, however, this passage gives no indication that finding oneself excluded from the wedding banquet is a permanent situation.

**3. Matthew 25:31-46**

Jesus said that when he returns and sits on his throne, the people of all nations will gather before him, with the righteous on the right hand side and the unrighteous on the left. Then he "[34]will say to those at his right hand, 'Come, you that are blessed by my Father, inherit the kingdom prepared for you from the foundation of the world,'" because of the many ways they had faithfully helped others and, in so doing, served him. To those at his left hand, however, he will say "[41]'You that are accursed, depart from me into the eternal fire prepared for the devil and his angels,'" because they had failed to serve anyone but themselves. He concludes by saying, "[46]these will go away into eternal punishment, but the righteous into eternal life."

In order to understand this passage, it is very helpful to consider the meaning of the Greek word *aionios*, which is translated "eternal." First of all, *aionios* does not apply only to the length of life. It is used in the Bible in reference to the quality of life, to accent the wonderful joy of heaven or the terrible misery of hell.

Secondly, if the writer of this passage had intended to communicate the concept of punishment without end, he could have used the word *aidios*, (meaning perpetual[1]) but he didn't. He used *aionios* instead, which means "age lasting."[2] "Age lasting" would not mean the same as "without end," but would last to the end of the age, however long that might be. By virtue of the definition of *aionios*, therefore, we can conclude that eternal punishment in hell will eventually come to an end.

**4. Luke 16:19-31**

Jesus told a parable of a rich man who lived a self-centered life, and a poor man named Lazarus, whom the rich man had neglected to help. They both died. Lazarus went to heaven and the rich man went to Hades. The rich man asked Abraham to send Lazarus to give him some water [24]"'for I am in agony in these flames.' [25]But Abraham said, 'Child, remember that during your lifetime you received your good things, and Lazarus in like manner evil things; but now he is comforted here, and you are in agony. [26]Besides all this, between you and us a great chasm has been fixed, so that those who might want to pass from here to you cannot do so, and no one can cross from there to us.'"

Let's remember that each parable Jesus told is meant to communicate primarily one main lesson. This one should not be considered an actual description of hades (hell) and heaven, including things such as a chasm that cannot be crossed. Rather, it communicates the understanding that those who make riches their god, and practice self-indulgence, will surely experience hell.

**5. 2 Thessalonians 1:5-9**

In this passage, the Apostle Paul states that, as evidence of God's righteous judgment, when Jesus returns from heaven he will inflict "[8]vengeance on those who do not know God and on those who do not obey the gospel of our Lord Jesus. [9]These will suffer the punishment of eternal destruction, separated from the presence of the Lord and from the glory of his might." This passage of Scripture, along with the others I have quoted, apparently supports the idea of hell in the next life, but there are legitimate reasons to conclude that, for an individual, hell is not necessarily without end.

## Scripture That Supports Universal Salvation

Many Bible passages suggest everyone will eventually be saved. Some of these passages are as follows:

**1. Matthew 18:21-22**

Peter asked Jesus, "[21]'Lord, if another member of the church sins against me, how often should I forgive? As many as seven times?' [22]Jesus said to him, 'Not seven times, but, I tell you, seventy-seven times.'" In other words, Jesus tells us there should be no end to our willingness to forgive others. Is it reasonable to think that God's forgiveness is limited? Is God less forgiving than God expects us to be? Surely not!

**2. Luke 15:3-6**

Jesus told the following parable: "[4]'Which one of you, having a hundred sheep and losing one of them, does not leave the ninety-nine in the wilderness and go after the one that is lost until he finds it? [5]When he has found it, he lays it on his shoulders and rejoices. [6]And when he comes home, he calls together his friends and neighbors, saying to them, 'Rejoice with me, for I have found my sheep that was lost.'" In this parable, the shepherd (God) was not content with 99 percent of his flock being saved, but looked for the one lost sheep until he found it. For God to stop looking for the lost sheep is to stop being God (love).

**3. John 12:32**

Jesus said, "I, when I am lifted up from the earth, will draw all people to myself." Being "lifted up from the earth" is a reference to Jesus' crucifixion, through which he will draw all people to himself (that is, save everyone).

**4. John 12:46-47**

Jesus stated, "[46]'I have come as light into the world, so that everyone who believes in me should not remain in the darkness. [47]I do not judge anyone who hears my words and does not keep them, for I came not to judge the world, but to save the world.'" Jesus came to save everyone in the world!

**5. Romans 5:18**

Paul the apostle wrote, "Therefore just as one man's trespass led to condemnation for all, so one man's act of righteousness leads to justification and life for all." Adam is the first man referred to in this passage. It was the result of his sin that all of humankind came to experience sinfulness, and thus condemnation. The second man refers to Christ. It was through his act of righteousness (dying on the cross) that leads to salvation for all. A passage similar to this is found in 1 Corinthians 15:22, where Paul writes, "For as all die in Adam, so all will be made alive in Christ."

**6. Romans 8:38-39**

Paul proclaimed, "[38]For I am convinced that neither death, nor life, nor angels, nor rulers, nor things present, nor things to come, nor powers, [39]nor height, nor depth, nor anything else in all creation, will be able to separate us from the love of God in Christ Jesus our Lord." Since nothing, including death, can separate us from the love of God, it's hard to imagine God not seeking release from hell for the people God loves.

**7. Philippians 2:10-11**

Paul wrote, "[10]At the name of Jesus every knee should bend, in heaven and on earth and under the earth, [11]and every tongue should confess that Jesus Christ is Lord." The phrase "under the earth" is a clear reference to the abode of the dead or hell. To "confess that Jesus Christ is Lord" was a phrase used in early baptismal services by which those being baptized expressed their commitment to Christ or declared that they had been saved through Christ.[3] To say that everyone under the

# Dare To Possess The Truth    11

earth (in hell) should bend their knee (bow humbly before Christ) and confess that Jesus Christ is Lord (profess salvation through Christ) is to affirm that it is possible for those in hell to be saved and that everyone in hell will eventually experience salvation.

## 8. Colossians 1:19-20

Paul declared regarding Christ, "[19]For in him all the fullness of God was pleased to dwell, [20]and through him God was pleased to reconcile to himself all things, whether on earth or in heaven, by making peace through the blood of his cross." God sent Jesus to rescue humanity. The good news is that God, through Christ, was pleased to reconcile to himself all things, including all humans.

## 9. 1 Timothy 2:4-6

Paul proclaimed, "[4](God) desires everyone to be saved and to come to the knowledge of the truth. [5]For there is one God; there is also one mediator between God and humankind, Jesus Christ, himself human, [6]who gave himself a ransom for all." Surely we can agree that God gets what God wants, since God is all-powerful. An affirmation of this truth is found in Job 42:1-2; "Then Job answered the Lord: 'I know that you can do all things, and that no purpose of yours can be thwarted.'" God is not a weakling. If God desires everyone to be saved, will God not succeed?

## 10. 1 John 2:1-2

The disciple, John, wrote, "[1]My little children, I am writing these things to you so that you may not sin. But if anyone does sin, we have an advocate with the Father, Jesus Christ the righteous; [2]and he is the atoning sacrifice for our sins, and not for ours only but also for the sins of the whole world." Jesus' atoning sacrifice was not just for a select group, but was for everyone.

## Making Our Decision

As we can see, there are passages of Scripture on both sides of this issue. How does one decide what is correct when there seems to be biblical support for both sides related to the question of universal salvation? To help discern the truth, we will consider many general biblical themes and profound implications in the next two lessons.

STUDY/DISCUSSION QUESTIONS:
1. How does it make you feel when you discover apparent inconsistencies in the Bible?
2. How do you decide what to believe when there seems to be biblical support for both sides of an issue?
3. How significant do you think it is that the Greek word *aionios* commonly translated "eternal" or "everlasting," means "age lasting"?
4. What would it be like if God did not have unlimited capacity to forgive those who turn to God?
5. What would the implications be if God ever stopped seeking the lost?
6. Is there any reason to conclude that God would not ultimately get what God wants?

# Lesson Three

# SEEING THE BIGGER PICTURE

## General Biblical Themes

To really understand what the Bible says regarding universalism it is very helpful to go beyond considering individual passages and look for general themes in the Bible that relate to the issue. Let's do that.

### Judgment

A theme which runs through the Bible is judgment, referred to in Hebrews 9:27; "It is appointed for mortals to die once, and after that the judgment." I believe the judgment scene is never one of a judge sitting on a throne who tells a trembling sinner that he or she is hell-bound, and informs others they are destined for heaven. Instead, we judge ourselves through our conscience in the light of God's love and mercy.

This understanding of judgment is reflected in Raymond A. Moody Jr.'s books, *Life After Life* and *Reflections on Life After Life*. He relates the many testimonies of people who had experienced clinical death and were later revived. Those with near-death experiences commonly reported experiencing an encounter with a being of light. They felt total and unconditional love and acceptance from this being of light whom many people identified as Christ. Moody writes, "The love and the warmth which emanate from this being to the dying person are utterly beyond words, and he feels completely surrounded by it and taken up in it, completely at ease and accepted in the presence of this being. He senses an irresistible magnetic attraction to this light."[1]

The being of light asked them questions, not in condemnation or accusation, but in a manner that helped them think about their lives. As a result, Moody discovered, "a kind of judgment took place, for in this state of heightened awareness, when people saw any selfish acts which they had done they felt extremely repentant. Likewise, when gazing upon those events in which they had shown love and kindness they felt satisfaction. It is interesting to note that the judgment in the cases I studied came not from the being of light, who seemed to love and accept these people anyway, but rather from within the individual being judged."[2]

The idea that people judge themselves is also represented in John 3:19-21, where Jesus says, "And this is the judgment, that the light has come into the world, and people loved darkness rather than light because their deeds were evil. For all who do evil hate the light and do not come to the light, so that their deeds may not be exposed. But those who do what is true come to the light, so that it may be clearly seen that their deeds have been done in God." This passage makes it clear to me that people themselves will decide whether they go to the light or darkness (heaven or hell). But I want to make it clear that if someone chooses to go to hell, it is not a final choice. I believe God will not let it be so.

Could heaven truly be heavenly for anyone if even one soul is forever forbidden from entering it? Even if being in hell is that person's own fault? There would always be a lingering sadness over those who were absent, who would never have a chance to experience the joys of heaven. If someone is in an accident and it is entirely his own fault, you don't refuse to take him to the hospital to be treated, do you? In the infinitely more important matter relating to a person's eternal welfare the same principle must surely apply. No matter how much the fault is our own (and to some extent it always is) the love of God will never cease trying to win us.

## The Grace of God

The concept of God's grace is one of the most dominant themes in the Bible. Grace is commonly defined as unmerited favor. Try as we might, we can never achieve God's standard of holiness and perfection, but God accepts and loves us anyway. This is expressed in Psalms 103:8,10,12; "[8]The Lord is merciful and gracious, slow to anger and abounding in steadfast love. . . . [10]He does not deal with us according to our sins, nor repay us according to our iniquities. . . . [12]as far as the east is from the west, so far he removes our transgressions from us." Ephesians 2:8-9 reads: "[8]For by grace you have been saved through faith, and this is not your own doing; it is the gift of God - [9]not the result of works, so that no one may boast."

If we insist that people must respond favorably to the gospel before they die in order to be saved, we have concluded that the grave is the end point of God's grace. It's clear to me that one cannot make a very convincing argument for that conclusion.

We can never wear down the grace of God. God's grace remains no matter what sins we commit. God does not hold a grudge. Neither does God demand justice or require us to do a prescribed amount of groveling before forgiving us. When we turn to God, we are accepted immediately and unconditionally because God has already acted in Christ to receive us. How can we entertain, even for a moment, the thought that God may be reluctant or slow to forgive us? God does not wait until we have paid the price, until we have been punished for our sins, before accepting us. Certainly, we experience the misery we have brought upon ourselves as a consequence of our behavior. But can you truly call that God's doing? God welcomes us home without regard for what we have done in the past, just as did the father in the story of the Prodigal Son.

Many people place much emphasis on the assumed rewards and punishments given by God. This gives more credence to justice than grace. Wouldn't it be arrogant of us to believe that a holy and just God, one who must punish sin, would let us go to heaven while condemning others to hell? If God operated strictly on the basis of justice, no one would be acceptable. The good news is that no one is so bad as to be beyond the possibility of experiencing salvation by grace.

## The Purpose of Punishment or Suffering

In an attempt to support their belief of endless punishment in hell, some people will say, "God is holy, and for that reason the punishment of evildoers is a moral necessity." In reality, while that may seem proper and just, the Bible presents us with an even higher standard. It teaches us that the ultimate moral necessity is that people be converted through punishment or suffering.

The purpose of biblical punishment is to make a wrongdoer a right-doer. If hell is endured without end, the experience would be of no value to an individual because there would be no chance of his embracing good, repenting and attempting a new beginning. Such a circumstance would be a travesty. Suffering from which nothing can be learned or gained is meaningless, and the one who brought it about would be a fiend, not a father. We as parents discipline our children, not for the sake of punishment, but in order to encourage change. Surely God is at least as honorable as any parent in this regard.

According to the Bible then, punishment (more specifically, suffering which we bring on ourselves as a direct consequence of our behavior) is never an end in itself, but is a means to bring about conversion. So we can properly conclude that hell has a useful purpose, whether it is the hell that we experience in this life or in the next. Its purpose is to help us realize the futility, hopelessness and meaninglessness of life without God. It helps us realize our need for God to save us. The ultimate end is not for God to punish sin but to eliminate the sin and, through conversion and transformation, save the sinner.

# God's Love

What could be a more important theme in the Bible than God's love? 1 John 3:7-9 declares, "Beloved, let us love one another, because love is from God; everyone who loves is born of God and knows God. Whoever does not love does not know God, for God is love. God's love was revealed among us in this way: God sent his only Son into the world so that we might live through him."

The belief that God is love presents a serious problem for those who also believe in endless punishment in hell. Once they think about it, not surprisingly, they confront a natural difficulty in reconciling the idea of a God whose love is limitless and unending, with the idea of a God who callously permits and even enforces endless punishment. One way out of their dilemma is to conclude that God's love is limited and conditional. For example, they may contend that God's love is either complacent or benevolent. Complacent love, according to them, is mandatory. It is love for someone who is morally upright. God would be obligated to love someone like Jesus, or a saint, for instance. On the other hand, they believe benevolent love is optional (the love for someone who is unworthy of love). With this way of thinking, they might decide that because people in hell are not praiseworthy, God has no obligation to love them. Though they accept that God is love, to them it does not seem necessary for God to love people who are in hell.

It's hard for me to comprehend how anyone could believe that God's love is optional. After all, the essence of God's grace is to love and forgive the unlovable. To believe that God's love is limited and conditional results in lowering God's status below humans. Humans have the ability to love those who are not worthy of love, and because of Christian teachings, feel somewhat of an obligation to do so. It is absurd to think that God could be less loving than humans.

## Expiation

Another of the Biblical themes, and one of its most powerful, is expiation. Expiation relates to the means by which atonement or reparation is made. We as humans are not able to make atonement for ourselves, so another way had to be provided. The Jews had come to believe that a sacrificial lamb made atonement. The New Testament takes us beyond that line of thinking with the advent of Jesus the Messiah. The significance of the Christian teaching regarding expiation is not that a Messiah, separate from God, made atonement for us. It was God who came to our rescue. God did not wait for us to demonstrate that we were worthy of God's love and salvation. Romans 5:8 reads, "God proves his love for us in that while we still were sinners Christ died for us."

Christ's death was not for the purpose of appeasing an angry God. Such an act would be pagan. Pagans in ancient times sometimes sacrificed their children to appease the angry god they feared. The Christian teaching is that we no longer need to try to appease God because it was God through Christ who provided the means for our salvation.

In 2 Corinthians 5:19 we read, "In Christ God was reconciling the world to himself, not counting their trespasses against them." 1 John 4:10 reads, "In this is love, not that we loved God but that he loved us and sent his Son to be the atoning sacrifice (expiation) for our sins." Never again should we think of God as an angry God whom we must try to appease. God does not look for reasons to condemn us, but never gives up looking for ways to get us to stop resisting so God can save us. Consistent with the expiation theme, in John 3:17, Jesus says, "Indeed, God did not send the Son into the world to condemn the world, but in order that the world might be saved through him." What good news that is!

## Jesus' Lack of Urgency

If Jesus believed the unsaved were destined to go to hell forever, I believe there would have been much greater urgency reflected in his ministry. I do not detect that kind of urgency in

Jesus as I read about him in the Bible. There were many times people turned away from Jesus, and he let them go. There is no indication that Jesus ever ran down the road after anyone to get him or her saved. He displayed unhurried patience, as if he had a lot of time. That kind of attitude is reflected in 2 Peter 3:8-9 which reads, "But do not ignore this one fact, beloved, that with the Lord one day is like a thousand years, and a thousand years is like one day. The Lord is not slow about his promise, as some think of slowness, but is patient with you, not wanting any to perish, but all to come to repentance."

## Life after Death

Many people hold to the belief that the devil is in hell with those who are lost, and God (Father, Son and Holy Spirit) is in heaven with those who are saved, and that arrangement will continue for eternity. John 14:2-3 seems to support this belief. It quotes Jesus as saying, "In my Father's house there are many dwelling places. If it were not so, would I have told you that I go to prepare a place for you? And if I go and prepare a place for you, I will come again and will take you to myself, so that where I am, there you may be also." Consequently, we Christians expect to dwell in heaven with Jesus, where together, we will live happily ever after.

I wonder if Jesus dwelling with us in heaven represents the whole picture of the next life. When Jesus lived among us, he spent a high percentage of his time with outcasts, tax collectors and sinners, to the extent that his actions seemed scandalous to the proper religious folks of his day. The Scriptures tell us; "Now all the tax collectors and sinners were coming near to listen to him. And the Pharisees and the scribes were grumbling and saying, 'This fellow welcomes sinners and eats with them'" (Luke 15:1-2).

In light of how Jesus lived when he walked among us, I believe it is totally logical to conclude that Jesus would not spend all of his time exclusively with people enjoying heaven while ignoring those who suffer in hell. Since "Jesus Christ is the same yesterday and today and forever" (Hebrews 13: 8), I believe that, as long as there are people in hell, Jesus will spend much time with them, offering them support, encouragement, healing, forgiveness, and wholeness. Of course, since Jesus is Spirit, he is not limited to ministering in one place at a time, but can exercise his love and power in both heaven and hell simultaneously.

We affirm that Jesus saves people from hell each time we recite the Apostles' Creed. The traditional version reads that Jesus was "crucified, dead and buried; He descended into hell." Why did Jesus descend into hell? It's been taught ever since the time of the early Church that Jesus descended into hell to preach the good news to the lost, to rescue them. Note what it says in 1 Peter 3:18-20; 4:6.

> [18]For Christ also suffered for sins once for all, the righteous for the unrighteous, in order to bring you to God. He was put to death in the flesh, but made alive in the spirit, [19]in which also he went and made a proclamation to the spirits in prison, [20]who in former times did not obey. . . .[6]For this is the reason the gospel was proclaimed even to the dead, so that, though they had been judged in the flesh as everyone is judged, they might live in the spirit as God does.

This passage makes it very clear that Jesus saves people from hell, because it makes specific reference to him having done so. I believe Jesus will never rest as long as anyone remains in hell. I am confident that countless Christians will join with Jesus, their leader, in a great mission to rescue those who suffer. And they will not quit, either, until the last person is liberated from hell.

STUDY/DISCUSSION QUESTIONS:
1.  What might cause you to believe God seeks you and others even when you are not aware of it?
2.  What does judgment mean to you?
3.  Do we choose our destination following death or does God decide?
4.  Is the grave the end point for God's grace?

5. What might cause you to think that God is just? Or unjust?
6. What's the purpose of hell?
7. What would the implications be if God's love were optional or conditional?
8. What does expiation mean to you?
9. How might Jesus and his followers rescue people from hell?

# Lesson Four

# AMAZING GRACE

## Implications Of Universal Salvation
## Versus Eternal Damnation

The most basic and profound of all issues pertaining to the Christian faith is whether God will eventually save everyone. Contemplation of this issue brings forth many questions, such as: Is God our advocate or our adversary? If God is against us, wouldn't we need someone to save us from God? On the other hand, if God is for us, who can prevent God from saving us all?

As you can see, the very integrity of God is at stake with the issue of whether or not God will eventually save everyone. We might wonder, is God really all loving, and merciful and gracious? Or, is God a highly judgmental God who holds a grudge for eternity against those who are either not good enough to deserve to go to heaven, or who did not receive salvation before they died?

## God is More Gracious than Humans

It is commonly accepted that God is gracious, loving and merciful. In spite of what the Bible says in support of God's gracious loving mercy, however, much of what passes as religion denies the existence of such a God. God is instead often understood as a moral force in the universe that rewards the good and punishes those who are evil. But if God's only function is to be a supernatural bookkeeper, recording everyone's behavior and rewarding or punishing accordingly, then where is God's grace?

People who reject the idea of a God of eternal damnation sometimes tell me that if it was their decision, they would have mercy on people suffering in hell, and they would forgive the sufferers when they repented and allow them into heaven. Then they go further, to say something like, "If God is less loving, merciful and forgiving than I am, and if God's thirst for vengeance is so insatiable that an eternity of torment will not satisfy it, I don't want to have anything to do with God." (And I cannot blame them.) A God of that nature is certainly not appealing or attractive, and would clearly seem to be of a much different nature than God as presented by Jesus, whom he called "Father" ["Abba," (Mark 14:36) which could appropriately be translated, "Daddy"].

While talking with people who believe in an everlasting punishment in hell, I have often asked the question, "If you were God, would you consign some people to hell and then abandon them forever?" Not one of those people has been willing to answer that question. Without exception, they have either refused to answer it all together or they have tried to avoid it by saying something like, "I'm not God, so it's not a valid question," or "It doesn't matter what I would do." They seem to realize very quickly that if they say they would abandon people in hell, it would make them seem very uncaring and hard-hearted. Of course, they do not perceive themselves in that way. They realize that if they were really honest with themselves they would have to answer, "No." They are smart enough to realize it presents a serious problem for them to say they would not abandon people in hell, while they contend that God would do so. That would mean they believe God is less compassionate than they are. Because they do not want to seem so foolish as to suggest God is morally and ethically inferior to them, they choose to avoid answering the original question.

As for myself, as imperfect as I am, I would never consider abandoning even one person to endless hell. It's hard for me to imagine that anyone else would do so either. Perhaps some of us would be inclined to abandon certain individuals for a while, but not forever. I cannot believe God is morally or ethically inferior to me or other humans, so I cannot believe God would abandon anyone in hell.

## God is More Gracious than Parents

If any of us continually and severely punished a child of our own for the rest of his life rather than listening to and acting on his pleas for mercy, we would either be put in jail or a mental hospital. Abuse happens all too often. People who are guilty of such offenses are locked up. How can we believe God would do something for which we mortals would be judged criminal or insane?

Sometimes a severely strained relationship develops between a child and his parents. Usually things can be worked out in a positive way, but occasionally the situation escalates to the extent that the parents, through an expression of "tough love," expel the child from their home. Even in an extreme situation this effort is not meant as a permanent expulsion. If a child truly changes and starts doing what is right, the parents normally welcome the child back into a new and positive relationship.

Surely there are parents in heaven whose children have very deservedly found themselves expelled from the fullness of life to suffer in hell. It is hard to imagine parents so hard-hearted as to deny the possibility of their children's transformation and release from hell, no matter how much difficulty their children might have given them. In fact, anybody worthy of dwelling in heaven will desire release from hell, not only for their own children, but also for their friends, neighbors, and even their enemies. Especially their enemies! According to Matthew 5:43-44, 46 Jesus says,

> [43]"You have heard that it was said, 'You shall love your neighbor and hate your enemy.' [44]But I say to you,

Love your enemies and pray for those who persecute you. . . [46]For if you love those who love you, what reward do you have? Do not even the tax collectors do the same?"

This passage makes it clear that loving one's enemies is what distinguishes Christians from non-Christians. Surely God steadfastly remains at least as loving, forgiving and accepting as any parent or any Christian in this life or the next.

## Gracious but Not Soft on Sin

Our affirmation of universal salvation does not mean we would suggest God is soft on sin. We all know sin is a terribly tragic thing. It causes people to experience hell. Sin is very serious, so serious that God sent his Son to save us from it. Because sin is so serious, we should be eternally grateful that God came to our rescue.

## Many Lack Opportunities to be Saved

Often people do not have a reasonable opportunity to experience salvation before they die. Many grow up in homes where there is no interest in the Church, or where there is outright hostility toward anything Christian. Some people suffer harsh experiences with the Church and, as a result, do not want to associate with Christians, often because of Christians' hypocrisy, where their actions are inconsistent with what they profess to believe. Others, as children, endure a bad relationship with their father and consequently, cannot bring themselves to love and serve a God whom people call "Father". Some people are led astray by cults and subjected to brainwashing. Still others go through life without hearing sufficiently of God's salvation.

So there are many, many valid reasons why people may not experience a fair opportunity to be saved before they die. If we think about it, we might ask, "What is to become of all of those people?" Surely God would not be so unreasonable and unfair as to consign them to suffer in hell forever on the technicality that they had not accepted salvation before their death!

By the same token, how about those who did apparently have many good opportunities to accept salvation during their lifetime, and for whatever reasons failed to do so? Is it fair or right that they be consigned to hell forever with no further opportunity for conversion? Even with many opportunities, who is to say that they received an adequate amount of exposure to the faith to result in conversion? In many cases, perhaps one more chance was all it might have taken for them to have accepted their salvation. Would God be so unreasonable as to deny them that one saving opportunity? Surely not!

There are religions other than Christianity. Is it possible to be saved through them? The billions of people around the world who have grown up under the influence of other religions again may not have had a fair chance to hear and respond favorably to the Christian gospel. Obviously, if they are saved through other religions, billions of people (non-Christians) will enter into heaven following death. But if they are not saved, they will all suffer in hell. If that is the case, could God be so uncaring as to forever deny release from hell even for those who faithfully followed their religious convictions in this life?

## Trying to Get God Off the Hook

If God consigns sinners to hell to suffer forever without any opportunity to make amends wouldn't that very idea suggest God is something of a monster? Those who believe in eternal damnation but are not willing to concede that God is a monster often seek to find ways to get God off the hook. Some even go to the extreme of maintaining that endless hell is a manifestation of God's love. Perhaps the most well known attempt to do this was by Dante in *The Inferno*.

*The Inferno* is Dante's perception of hell. In his writing, incorrigible sinners were so tortured because of their own evil it was not deemed necessary or appropriate for external punishment to be imposed upon them, the way hell is usually perceived. Justice allowed sinners to suffer only from what they brought on themselves due to their sinful condition, and no more. However, if they were exposed to the holy light of God's unveiled presence they suffered more greatly. Therefore, according to Dante's view, because God continued to love everyone, even those who had rebelled against God, God provided hell as a refuge from God's presence. It was not out of wrath or vengeance that God created hell, but it was done as a result of God's unending love for all people. According to this way of thinking, "God could not remove the inherent pain of evil being, but he could and did provide a refuge from a greater pain. And so justice and love built hell, the painful refuge."[1]

Even though this explanation is seemingly well intentioned, I believe it is a very inadequate attempt to get God off the hook. It amounts to a rationalization those believers of eternal damnation use to prove that God is not a monster even though God is perceived by them to do monstrous things. Wouldn't it be better for all of us to give up the monstrous misunderstanding about God and eternal damnation in hell so it would be no longer necessary for us to rationalize?

## Christ's Victory Is Complete

Interestingly, I have found some variations in the beliefs held among theologians and Church leaders who espouse universal salvation. As an example, some teach that hell is experienced only in this life. They declare that Christ has provided salvation for everyone, whether they realize it and accept it or not. Thus, they teach that there will be no hell after death and everyone will go to heaven because of Christ's victory.

I agree that Christ's victory is universal and complete. But, I cannot accept the non-existence of hell after death. The Bible teaches us about hell in the next life as well as in this life. Many people are still rejecting God at the time of their death, so they are presumably destined for hell unless they are to become converted immediately following death. I believe this probably happens with many people, though I am not aware of any biblical teaching that suggests this will be the case with everyone. Consequently, I must conclude that even though salvation through Christ is complete, some people, while not realizing they are saved, will continue to live as though they are lost and thus, experience hell until they are converted. I believe God will eventually help everyone realize and accept that Christ has already provided salvation for them, and lead them to heaven, including, when necessary, to save people from hell.

STUDY/DISCUSSION QUESTIONS:
1. What might cause you to believe that God is either for us or against us?
2. Could there be an end to God's mercy and grace?
3. What would it say about a person if they were willing to consign some people to hell forever?
4. How much exposure to the Christian faith is sufficient to make a person responsible for accepting or rejecting it?
5. Will those who faithfully follow other religions go to heaven? Why? Or why not?
6. Do you ever feel the need to get God off the hook?
7. What do you think about the idea that everyone is already saved even though many do not yet realize it?

# Lesson Five

# I WANT TO DO IT MYSELF

## Do We Have Free Will?

We all like to believe we are in charge of our lives, that we can take care of ourselves. We have been taught to be self-sufficient and to not accept charity because to do so reflects weakness and dishonor. This way of thinking has become so deeply ingrained in some of us that we might even feel uneasy about accepting a gift offered us by a friend. Our self-sufficiency also carries over into our religious beliefs where it causes us to conclude that, of our own free will, we are able to save ourselves.

Ephesians 2:8-9 says, "For by grace you have been saved through faith, and this is not of your own doing; it is the gift of God - not the result of works, so that no one may boast." Even though this passage makes it clear that we are saved by grace instead of good works, many of us still find great difficulty in accepting that free gift. We want very much to earn our salvation.

Some people put much emphasis on free will. Obviously, we do have freedom. We make choices every day. But are we totally free? That is the question we must address as we deal with the issues of how we are saved and whether anyone might spend eternity in hell.

## God Will Prevail

I get the impression that some people are not particularly bothered by the prospect that certain other people might be consigned to hell forever. They explain, "As I see it, some people choose to be saved so they can get in to heaven. Others choose to reject God. Because of that, they should go to hell. It's too bad, but it's a choice they made of their own free will." It is as if they are saying, "I had the good sense to get myself saved, and if other people are not as wise as me, well, too bad."

It makes me ask, are some people saved only because they use good sense? Does this also mean others go to hell because they freely make bad choices? I believe the only reason we are able to choose salvation is because of our being drawn to God by God's grace and power. And the only reason we might reject God is because we are frightened, misguided people. Because some people continue to reject God, they go to hell after they die. But I believe God does not simply give up on them. So, while we do have free will to a degree, we do not possess it to the extent that we can resist God forever. It is not logical, nor is there anything in the Bible that might lead us to believe that any human would be able to resist forever the advances, the wooing of Almighty God, the creator. Is the creature ever more powerful than the creator?

Do we have total free will? Are we completely free to make choices that result in either happiness or misery? Obviously, we sometimes do things that cause us pain. Are these totally free choices or are they the result of influences (such as alcoholism, drug addiction or difficult family situations) that are often beyond our control? If we have complete free will to make choices, as some people suggest, wouldn't it be illogical for us to choose to live in a way that would cause us to experience hell? And if we continue to have freedom of choice in the next life, wouldn't it be utterly absurd to choose to continue to suffer in hell forever? The alternative would be to accept the joy, peace, and forgiveness (the eternal life) that God by grace continually offers. Choosing eternal life is an easy choice, it seems to me. That is, if we really do have complete free will.

On the other hand, what if people do not have total freedom? What if there are negative influences that compel us to sometimes go astray or make bad choices? If that is the case, would God condemn misguided people to hell forever, or would God overcome those negative forces and save everyone? Both the Bible and logic tell us, yes; God would do so.

## Salvation for the Worst of Sinners

Some people are sympathetic to the teaching of universal salvation, and want to affirm it. But they find difficulty with the idea that notorious sinners or criminals could ever be saved. Short of denying free will all together for those wretched sinners who have the propensity to repeatedly make bad choices, some people cannot imagine those unfortunate souls ever being saved.

The important truth we need to keep in mind here is that no one is more powerful than God. No one can resist God's grace forever. We are like children trying to dam up a rushing mountain stream before it can water the valley below. We may be successful for a while, but the waters keep rising against the rocks. Inevitably, the water surges over the dam and tumbles down to the valley where it quenches the thirst of all who wait for it. Surely we can see that when God combines a steady stream of love and grace with as much time as this process takes to convert each person, God will prevail in any quest to save even the most hardened sinner.

Happily, we are all destined for salvation. That which is destined is something over which we have no choice and which we cannot prevent. By definition, our destiny is in God's hands and is predetermined by God. Whether we like it or not, or believe it or not, or even work with all our might against it, we cannot stop God from saving everyone.

## God Is Not a Monster

Does God allow some people to condemn themselves forever of their own free will? Noted contemporary author,

Robert Short, states in his book, *Something To Believe In,* that if that were the case it would make God one kind of monster or another. "He is either the weak God of unlimited love but limited power, or else he is the cruel God of unlimited power but limited love."[1]

The weak God who possesses unlimited love but limited power would choose to limit God's own power in order to give people free will, supposedly out of love. Such a God could then only helplessly stand by as God's children freely damn themselves. Wouldn't that be like the father who told his young child to stay in the yard and then did nothing more while his child walked onto the street to be killed when he was struck by a passing car? Surely any loving earthly father would do everything he could to prevent harm from coming to his child. Certainly God would do the same. We make God to be a monster if we believe God would not use God's great power to save all of us, but would instead say something like, "It's his own fault. He knew what he was doing. It's just too bad he disobeyed me."

With the second kind of monster, God possesses unlimited power but limited love. This kind of God resembles an eight hundred pound gorilla that can do whatever he wants. No one can stop him. Here there is no pretense that people have been given free will. God is totally in charge, although not necessarily being guided or restrained by love. God, according to this way of thinking, consigns most people to eternal damnation without any regret, and saves only a chosen few.

The teaching of eternal damnation makes it impossible to believe that God is both all loving and all-powerful, but necessitates that God be one or the other type of monster Gods. Neither of these two images of God is particularly appealing, or supported by Scripture.

## The Idolatry of Free Will
It is of great significance that when Jesus was on the cross, he did not pray, saying, "Father, throw them all into hell because they have free will and they know very well what they

are doing." Instead, he said, "Father, forgive them; for they do not know what they are doing" (Luke 23:34). This Scripture suggests we do not have total free will, but it makes it clear we are forgiven. Believing that we are saved by free will denies Scripture. According to the book of John, Jesus says, "No one can come to me unless drawn by the Father who sent me" (John 6:44).

Most importantly, the doctrine of free will denies God and results in idolatry, of worshipping and trusting oneself instead of God. Not completely trusting in God, people tend to resist placing the all-important matter of whether they end up in heaven or hell entirely in God's hands. This position can be expressed in Robert Short's words, as follows: "Please step aside, God. In this little matter of where we're going to spend eternity, we'll decide ourselves with our own 'free wills', thank you!"[2] May we all avoid this kind of idolatry. Short further says, "All do-it-yourself salvation schemes are actually either unconscious or disguised atheism."[3] Ultimately, do-it-yourself-ers trust in themselves rather than in God for their salvation.

## The Irresistible God

If we are not saved because of making good decisions by our free will, but God saves us by acting irresistibly, does that mean we have lost our freedom? John Wesley, the founder of the Methodist movement in the eighteenth century, said that is not the case. In fact, he claimed that everyone in the world could be saved without the loss of liberty, according to a sermon entitled, "The General Spread of The Gospel," which he preached on April 22, 1783. He said that a city, nation, or the whole world could become Christian, and that it could take place without difficulty if only we suppose that God acts irresistibly. It would be as when God created the world. God said, "Let there be light" (Genesis 1:3) and there was light.

Wesley then went on to tell the listeners that, when they were converted, God did not take away their understanding but it was enlightened and strengthened; God did not destroy their affections but they were made more vigorous than before; God did not take away their liberty, their power of choosing between good and evil; God did not force them but because of being assisted by God's grace they chose the better way. "Now in the same manner as God *has* converted so many to himself without destroying their liberty, he *can* undoubtedly convert whole nations, or the whole world. And it is as easy to him to convert a world as one individual soul."[4]

Some people speak of human freedom as if it is the highest of all values. They are even willing to consign countless people to endless hell in order to maintain the doctrine of free will. But, in the end, I believe there is a higher standard involved here than whether or not people have total free will or liberty. Isn't it more important that people be saved than that their freedom be left totally intact? We have already established that God can save the whole world without violating our free will. But even if that were not the case, surely a loving God would interfere with human freedom in certain ways if it were necessary in order to prevent anyone from becoming eternally lost.

There are at least two situations in which humans would feel justified in interfering with the freedom of others. We, first of all, would feel justified in preventing one person from doing harm to another. Because of this, a loving father might report his own son to the police in an effort to prevent him from committing a crime. We would also feel justified in preventing others from doing great harm to themselves. So a parent might even physically restrain his or her child in an effort to prevent him from injuring himself. Just as loving parents would restrict the freedom of their children, so too we can be sure that if it were necessary, God would restrict the freedom of the children God loves in order to save them.

So the reality of the situation is that we humans have free will, and we use it to make many decisions every day. But we do not have total freedom when it comes to the issue of where we will spend eternity. A loving God could never have created a world in which we, through our free will, would have the capacity to damn ourselves for eternity. Instead, even in our freedom, God guides us all into union with Godself.

STUDY/DISCUSSION QUESTIONS:
1. Why might we want to save ourselves?
2. What degree of free will do we have?
3. How long can you resist God?
4. Do some people's beliefs make God into a monster?
5. What might cause people to want to trust in themselves instead of God for salvation?
6. Would you ever not want God to be in charge of your life?
7. By what means might God save everyone without violating anyone's free will?
8. How would you feel about it if God interfered with your freedom in order to save you?

# Lesson Six

# LAYING A SOLID FOUNDATION

## What God Is Like

What we believe about God is the foundation of our faith. The rest of our religious beliefs are built upon those underpinnings. If our understanding of God is naive, antiquated or reflects only part of what the Bible says, then our other religious beliefs will inevitably be misguided. But if our perception of God is more nearly complete and enlightened, then the rest of what we believe will be enlightened also.

To help us in our understanding of God, I'd like to begin with early Old Testament thinking and follow the progression of thought into the New Testament, especially focusing on the words of Jesus.

### Family Deity

In very early Old Testament times, each family or tribe believed they had their own god. So, according to Exodus 3:1-5, when God appeared to Moses in a burning bush to call him to lead the Israelites out of their slavery in Egypt and on to the Promised Land, Moses asked God to identify himself. He needed to determine which god he was speaking to from among the many gods that were perceived to exist in that day. He knew he would have to tell the Israelites who had sent him.

God replied, "Thus you shall say to the Israelites, 'The LORD, the God of your ancestors, the God of Abraham, the God of Isaac, and the God of Jacob, has sent me to you'" (Exodus 3:15). As we can see, God was initially perceived to be a very exclusive god, relating only to one family or tribe.

## Wizard of Oz

As the centuries passed the prophets helped people come to realize there is only one God, the God who created the universe and who is the God of all nations. They generally thought of God as the Supreme Being who lives somewhere out beyond the world; the God who set everything in motion, and periodically intervenes in the running of the world or in people's lives; the God who they expected to send a Messiah to earth like a visitor from above to provide salvation for humankind.

This is what I would call the Wizard of Oz perception of God. According to this understanding, God is perhaps a kindly old gentleman with gray hair and a long beard, who sits up in heaven with all of his knowledge and wisdom, and pulls strings to dramatically demonstrate his awesome power.

## Spirit

Well before the end of Old Testament times and the birth of Jesus, the Israelites began to move beyond the Wizard of Oz understanding of God. This was done for practical reasons. They wondered, for example, if God resided in heaven, how could God hear and answer prayers from everyone all over the world at the same time? There had to be a better way to perceive what God is like. They began to realize that God is spirit, that God could be everywhere and relate with everyone at the same time.

Hebrew, the language of the ancient Israelites, helped them to comprehend what God as spirit means. The Hebrew word *ruach* relates three meanings; wind, breath and spirit. The Israelites came to understand that God's spirit was like the air we breathe or like the blowing of the wind. They realized that, like the air or wind, God was not visible, yet was the source of life and that you could be aware of God's power when God acts.

In building on this theme Jesus said, "The wind blows where it chooses, and you hear the sound of it, but you do not know where it comes from or where it goes. So it is with everyone who is born of the Spirit" (John 3:8). Jesus further said, "God is spirit, and those who worship him must worship in spirit and truth" (John 4:24). After Jesus rose from the dead, he met with his disciples and "he breathed on them and said to them, 'Receive the Holy Spirit'" (John 20:22).

Thinking of God as spirit is very helpful in understanding how God can be with each of us at the same time. That is certainly something we can affirm and celebrate. God is not just the Almighty who created the universe but is as close to us as the air we breathe and loves us more than we can even comprehend. God sent Jesus to be our Savior, so we can have fullness of life now and go to be with God forever after we die.

## Oneness with Humankind

What we have established so far is that God as the Creator is as far away as the most distant galaxy. At the same time, God is very close to us and we can even appropriately think of God as coming into us as the air we breathe and also as living in our hearts. But with this perception, God is still considered a different kind of being from humans, and one who is completely separate from humans. There are some passages of Scripture, however, which indicate that God is not completely different or separate from us.

Jesus, when he walked among us as a human, was not totally different or separate from God. He said, "The Father and I are one" (John 10:30), and "The Father is in me and I am in the Father" (John 10:38). If Jesus as a human enjoyed that kind of relationship with God, why would it not also be true of the rest of us? Many will say Jesus was different because he was not only human but divine as well. There are indications Jesus did not see it that way.

Jesus told his followers, "The kingdom of God is within you" (Luke 17:21). Also, according to John 17:20-21, Jesus said in prayer for his followers, "I ask not only on behalf of these, but also on behalf of those who will believe in me through their word, that they may all be one. As you, Father, are in me and I am in you, may they also be in us." Jesus does claim to be one with God, but he also says that the same is true of us. So Jesus does not set himself apart from other humans, and he encourages us to affirm our oneness with God and to live powerfully and victoriously in that relationship.

## Love

The ultimate understanding in regard to what God is like is to recognize that God is love. Some people not only affirm that God is love, but go to the extreme of contending that love is God. While I appreciate what they are saying and believe there is some validity to it, I cannot go that far myself. It seems to me that in saying that love is God one runs into pretty much the same difficulty as we do with pantheism, which means that God is everything and everything is God. In both cases, we limit what God can be. With pantheism we are saying God exists only as a part of the physical universe. In saying that love is God we limit God to existing only as love. So I would not go so far as to say that love is God. But we can and must conclude that God is love, and what a powerful affirmation that is.

We are told in John 3:16, "For God so loved the world that he gave his only Son, so that everyone who believes in him may not perish but may have eternal life." Also, 1 John 4:7-8, 16 states, "Beloved, let us love one another, because love is from God; everyone who loves is born of God and knows God. Whoever does not love does not know God, for God is love. . . Those who abide in love abide in God, and God abides in them."

To assert that God is love is to believe that when we experience love we are in touch with God. Matthew 18:20 reads, "Where two or three are gathered in my name, I am there among them." Not only does this mean that Jesus (or God) is present as an additional person, but is there and is experienced in the expressions of love between people.

## More Thoughts About God

Now I would like to share some other important thoughts regarding what God is like. First of all, we must move beyond 1,000 B.C. in our understanding of God. Before that time, God was perceived to be a family, tribal or national deity. If we can go beyond that antiquated view of God we will be able to realize that no one possesses God. God is not just the God of Abraham, or the Israelites, or even Christians, but of everyone. No one has exclusive rights to God's grace. God's grace is not just for the benefit of Christians, for them alone to possess, but it is a universal gift God shares with the world.

The Bible makes it very clear that God is love. Any teaching that denies or minimizes that love runs contrary to the Bible. So, teaching that God locks people in hell and throws away the key has to be faulty. Claiming that God loves only the lovable or that God does not love those who are in hell must be seriously questioned. And saying God loves Billy Graham more than Adolf Hitler must be challenged. After all, who needs the transforming power of unconditional love more than Hitler? For God to withhold love from anyone would amount to admitting defeat. It is through the power of unconditional love that ultimate victory will be achieved.

Since God is in us and we are in God and we are one with God, nothing can separate us from God. For God to abandon anyone in hell would amount to God abandoning Godself. That is impossible for God to do. God is not just a detached, high and mighty being who pronounces judgments on people from a distance. Instead, God is the ground of our being, the meaning of our existence, far away and intimately close, powerful and gentle, saving and loving. God is not hostile but friendly.

Over the centuries the Church has largely lost its appreciation of the fact that the Scriptures say God is in us and we are in God, we are one with God and we are participants of the divine nature. According to L. Robert Keck, author of *Sacred Eyes*, "We have created a chasm between the sacred and the profane, heaven and earth, divine and human, spirit and matter, good and evil."[1] Because of this, we naturally have the perception that the Divine resides beyond ourselves in God or a Savior, and that humans, by comparison, are a pretty sorry lot.

By projecting attention outward away from ourselves rather than recognizing the divinity that God has put within each of us, we diminish all of humankind that is made in God's image. It also prevents us from developing our God-given potential by God's grace and help, which in turn keeps us from experiencing heaven to its fullest. This low view of humankind also makes it possible to label some people as trash, sinners, lost, ungodly, hopeless, unworthy of heaven, and deserving of hell. With that understanding, without a tear in their eyes, some people feel completely justified when they mentally consign certain others to hell forever.

What a difference it makes when we can really grasp that God has made each one of us to be very special, and understand that we are all his precious children, made in God's image and partakers of the divine nature. Then we will not be able to tolerate the thought of one lost soul. Then the tears will flow from our eyes as they did from Jesus when he wept over the city of Jerusalem (Luke 19:41). Then we will not be content until the last precious soul has entered heaven. We will join in spirit with the good shepherd who was not content that 99 out of his hundred sheep were safe, but kept looking until the last one was found (Luke 15:3-7).

Finally, we will then be able to understand why the father of the prodigal son kept longing, yearning and looking for his lost son to come home. When he finally arrived home he said, "'Quickly, bring out a robe – the best one – and put it on him; put a ring on his finger and sandals on his feet. And get the fatted calf and kill it, and let us eat and celebrate; for this son of mine was dead and is alive again; he was lost and is found!'" (Luke 15:22-24).

STUDY/DISCUSSION QUESTIONS:
1.  Whose side is God on in times of war?
2.  What are the implications of *ruach* meaning wind, breath and spirit?
3.  What does it mean that we are one with God? Is it true only of Christians or everyone?
4.  God is love. In what respects is that true? What is love?
5.  What does God's unconditional love for everyone mean to you?
6.  How do you understand the idea that God is the ground of our being?
7.  What does it mean that we have been made in God's image?

# Lesson Seven

# FREE AT LAST

## From Hell To Heaven - How It Is Accomplished

It is important for us to clearly understand what would be involved in moving from an existence in hell to an eternity in heaven. I caution you against thinking that, if getting out of hell is an option and if everyone is eventually going to be saved anyway, you can live it up now, because if you do end up in hell, you will easily be able to just leave and find your way to heaven. I must strongly emphasize that you cannot get out of hell in the same way as if you were traveling from one town to another.

### Heaven and Hell - Spiritual States of Being

The environment of hell is not necessarily different from that of heaven, but what one does within it is what makes it heaven or hell. People commonly have the impression that dying and going to heaven is like moving to Hawaii. The assumption is that one could not help but be happy while living in such a paradise. If we give it some thought, however, we will realize such a scenario really could not be true. There are unhappy people in Hawaii, as is true any place else. And there are people living in severe climates who experience great happiness and fulfillment. So it is not particularly relevant what the environment is like in heaven, or hell.

Hell is not so much a place as it is a spiritual state of being; a state characterized by such things as hatred, selfishness, greed, revenge, anger, feuding and power struggles. By everyone living according to those standards it makes it hell for everybody living there. The real issue is not that people will exist in hell, but that hell will exist within them. That means, you cannot leave hell anymore than you can leave yourself because that which makes it hell comes from inside you.

We can appropriately conclude that God did not create hell as if it were in a geographical location such as Siberia where a person might be sent for punishment. It is more accurate to consider hell the creation of sinners, because sinfulness results in misery. I believe that no one is sent to hell to be punished for his or her sins. Hell is merely the natural consequence of the behavior with which we hurt others or ourselves. When we hurt others, the pain eventually comes back to cause misery for ourselves.

## Change That Results in Heaven

While you cannot leave hell as if you were going from one geographical location to another, you can get out of hell in another sense. You can be delivered from hell by allowing God to change what is within you, to turn you around so that your existence will be characterized not by hatred but love; not by selfishness but selflessness; not by greed but generosity; not by revenge but forgiveness; not by anger but compassion; not by feuding but peace; and not by power struggles, but by submitting to God's power. When a person is changed in that way, or turned around (converted), he or she will no longer experience hell but heaven.

This kind of change is not something that happens automatically or easily. For one thing, people have a sinful nature that causes them to go astray and seek life from other gods. Some of these gods are obvious, such as materialism, power and pleasure. Other less obvious gods from which we might seek fullness in this life could be worthwhile causes or relationships with other people. This is not to suggest that we should not pursue worthwhile causes and relationships with others. It is just that if we depend on them for ultimate fulfillment and life, they will sometimes let us down.

There are many other factors, such as pride, self-idolatry, stubbornness, and misguidance that result in the experience of hell. They cause people to be deceived and led astray from God's purposes for life. As long as this deception continues to influence us, it will be no easier to get out of hell than it is to get out of a vicious cycle of revenge or to conquer a drug addiction.

## There Is Hope

Even with all that is against us, there is hope. This hope is in the power of an all-loving God, one who is much more powerful than any influence of evil upon us or our misguided nature. Whether it happens in this life or the next, people will eventually realize that their false gods have failed them; that instead of giving them fullness of life, and the promise of eternal life, their gods' failures have left them with despair and meaninglessness (hell). When that happens, people will become receptive to the one true God who will then lead them home to be with God, where they will experience eternal life. (Incidentally, that same process, which is conversion, takes place in this life as well as the next.)

For people who have not been converted in this life, the conversion process may take some time; an hour, a day, a year; perhaps a hundred years, or even longer. But I believe God will eventually prevail. God will help everyone see the light, and thereby draw them out of hell. God wants everybody to be saved. And I believe God will eventually succeed in saving everyone, more likely sooner than later.

## Prepare for Heaven

Let us think more about the consequences of our behavior. Let no one be deceived. Living in an evil way does not give us the best of this life or the next. It brings misery. Ultimately, it is hell. Besides, living according to evil standards actually prepares us for hell instead of heaven.

It would be wiser for us to establish patterns of life and values that prepare us for life in heaven. If we, for example, put all of our time and energy into getting rich, achieving academic accomplishments, climbing the social ladder, or doing better than the Joneses, it will not prepare us for heaven. If, on the other hand, we put our emphasis on endeavors, such as; trying to serve other people, comforting the distressed, helping those who are troubled and working for the unity of all humankind, we will become prepared to fit right into heaven in the next world. It does not make sense to subject us to the misery of hell at all, in this life or the next. So we are all well advised to humbly and faithfully serve God and help others now, and to allow God to give us victory in life. Then we will experience a degree of heaven in this life and become prepared to experience the fullness of heaven in the next life as well.

## The Command to Love

A Pharisee had asked Jesus which was the greatest commandment in the law. Jesus replied, "'You shall love the Lord your God with all your heart, and with all your soul, and with all your mind.' This is the greatest and first commandment. And a second is like it: 'You shall love your neighbor as yourself'" (Matthew 22:37-39).

This is the most basic teaching in Christianity. Love. When we love God and others we will experience the joy of their love and goodwill in return. That is the essence of salvation. It is eternal life. It is heaven, in this life and the next. On the other hand, living in a self-centered way, caring neither for God nor others is what it means to be lost. Such a life would cause us to experience hell, in this life and the next.

As we grow in our love for God and others, we will come to realize that the ultimate expression of love is to love our enemies. An impossible task, you might think, when you read Jesus as quoted in Matthew 5:43-45: "You have heard that it was said, 'you shall love your neighbor and hate your enemy.' But I say to you, Love your enemies and pray for those who persecute you, so that you may be children of your Father in heaven; for he makes his sun rise on the evil and on the good, and sends rain on the righteous and on the unrighteous." To seemingly make matters worse, this passage concludes with, "Be perfect, therefore, as your heavenly Father is perfect" (Matthew 5:48).

At first it may seem like there is no obvious connection between this concluding verse and the rest of the foregoing passage. First it says God is accepting of everyone, the evil as well as the good. Then it suggests we need to be perfect in order to be acceptable. Walter Wink (seminary professor and author), however, says, "Jesus could not have said, 'Be perfect.' There is no such word, or even concept, in Aramaic or Hebrew."[1]

Rather than describing moral perfection, "perfect" was an aesthetic term that could be used to describe a geometric form, for instance. In understanding the literal intent of the word within the context of this entire passage, it becomes clear that when Jesus says we are to behave like God, he is not saying that we are to be morally perfect (which is impossible). Instead, we are to mimic God in our love for even those who are least worthy of our love, our enemies. Loving even our enemies is entirely possible because Jesus calls and empowers us to embrace everyone. He is not calling us to an impossible perfection. As by grace we grow in God's love, we begin to understand that by recognizing and accepting our own imperfection, failures, and sinfulness, we will become enabled to embrace those whom we feel are least perfect, least deserving, and most threatening to us. We are to love God and others, even our enemies, and thus, experience salvation. Loving in that way demonstrates we have truly been converted.

That leads me to ask, what is the primary purpose of Christian conversion? It seems to me that most people believe the main reason we need to be converted is in order to get into heaven. I disagree. I believe the primary purpose of Christian conversion is to enable us to love as God loves. We naturally love those who love us, our family and friends. But Jesus says, "If you love those who love you, what reward do you have? Do not even the tax collectors do the same?" (Matthew 5:45). Christians are distinguished from the rest of humanity not because they are destined for heaven but because they have been empowered to love in a new way, to love strangers, persecutors, enemies, and the unlovable. If we learn to love in that way, the question of whether or not we will go to heaven will be of little significance. We will already be there.

## About-Face

The difference between an existence in heaven and one in hell is determined by the direction we are facing spiritually. Jeremiah 2:27 reads; "They have turned their backs on me, and not their faces." Those of us who are following God's ways are ultimately being drawn into an ever closer spiritual fellowship with God and those around us, and are thus experiencing heaven. Those who have turned away from God and the love of others to live a life concerned only with themselves experience the hell of alienation.

Some in heaven experience a greater degree of joy and fulfillment than others, depending on how close they have grown to God and those around them. By the same token, the degree of misery that one may experience in hell is determined by how far one has degenerated into the hell of self-indulgence, jealousy and revenge. Heaven and hell are not fixed states experienced by everyone in the same way. Instead, they are dynamic and changing, with each individual moving along a continuum of joy and pain, either closer to or further from the love of God and others.

To be drawn by God from hell to heaven is to allow oneself to be turned around (converted). This results in a person's removal from the continuum of hell, where people have turned their backs on God and others, to be placed on the continuum of heaven, where they experience the joy of face-to-face, loving encounters with God and others. It is like traveling home by way of an interstate highway when you realize you have taken a wrong turn, which resulted in your heading in the opposite direction from what you intended. To make matters worse, you are approaching dangerous storm clouds. You take the first opportunity to cross the median and head back the other way. Soon the sun is shining. What a joy it is to be on the way home!

That is the kind of change that places a person on the way of Jesus, who said, "I am the way. . .to the Father" (John 14:6), and identifies one with those "belonging to the Way" (Acts 9:2). The term, "the Way", suggests that there is no immediate and complete transformation, causing the person to have arrived. But it places the person on the right track, facing in the right direction, to begin an eternity of growth in grace. And what an adventure that is, as we experience more and more of God's grace and love!

We will address this great opportunity for growth in lesson nine.

STUDY/DISCUSSION QUESTIONS:
1. Why does God allow people to experience hell?
2. Is it helpful to you to think about heaven and hell being spiritual states of being?
3. Why is it so hard to break the cycle of sinful living?
4. What is heaven? And hell?
5. How might we learn to love our enemies?
6. Why not live it up now if everyone is going to be saved in the end anyway?
7. How do you understand conversion?

Lesson Eight

# GOING BEYOND WISHFUL THINKING

## The Power of Unconditional Love

What great news we have! We will all eventually be converted, transformed, and enabled to live in a new way. How can God accomplish such a feat? It is by the power of unconditional love. To identify the powerful love into which we are called, the writers of the New Testament used the Greek word *agape*. *Agape* is unselfish, spiritual love of one person for another, corresponding to the love of God for people.

### Unconditional Love Is Essential

The teaching of eternal damnation makes it impossible for us to believe that God loves us unconditionally. If we believe God consigns some people to hell forever, or simply abandons them in their misery, could we say with any conviction that God has unconditional love for us?

If we believe in eternal damnation, wouldn't that also mean we believe there is no such thing as unconditional love? If we think God lacks the capacity to love unconditionally, how could any of us expect to express it to others ourselves? Surely none of us would believe we are superior to God in the purity of our love. This would eliminate the possibility of unconditional love for God or ourselves, but isn't unconditional love exactly what we want and need in our lives? If, on the other hand, we embrace the teaching of universal salvation, haven't we recognized that unconditional love is not only possible, but that it is the force that is essential to bring about the salvation of everyone?

Just because God is unconditionally loving and accepting, it does not mean that our behavior lacks importance. Standards and behavior matter enormously. But rather than deserving love because we are righteous, it is precisely our condition as sinners that makes unconditional love essential. Only by its power and influence are people transformed to higher and higher standards.

What power is there in "be-good-and-you'll-be-rewarded religion" or "don't-be-bad-or-you'll-be-punished religion"? Either type provides us with only external motivation. Neither one brings about change within a person. Those kinds of religion amount to bargaining with God, and you get only what you bargained for. In contrast, there is enormous power in a "you-are-loved-unconditionally faith". The significance of this belief is that it has the power to transform each of us. The resulting internal changes provide the foundation for our new, victorious lives.

I realize this goes against conventional wisdom, which contends that God must punish evildoers. But that is not God's way. God's way is to unconditionally love evildoers.

## Jesus' Transforming, Unconditional Love

Unconditional love and acceptance is precisely what Jesus taught and demonstrated while he walked among us. Jesus was accepting, loving and forgiving (to a fault, as the Pharisees saw it). One day some people took a paralyzed man to Jesus so that Jesus might heal him. Even before he healed the man physically, Jesus said, "Friend, your sins are forgiven you" (Luke 5:20). What an amazing and revolutionary thing to do! He pronounced the man forgiven even before he had a chance to repent or do anything else to show he deserved forgiveness.

Wasn't that just like Jesus? As a result of actions such as this, sinners were empowered to live as forgiven people. Think of the implications!

One day while Jesus passed through Jericho a man named Zacchaeus climbed up in a tree to get a better look at Jesus. As Jesus approached, he looked up and said,

> "Zacchaeus, hurry and come down; for I must stay at your house today." [6]So he hurried down and was happy to welcome him. [7]All who saw it began to grumble and said, "He has gone to be the guest of one who is a sinner." [8]Zacchaeus stood there and said to the Lord, "Look, half of my possessions, Lord, I will give to the poor; and if I have defrauded anyone of anything, I will pay back four times as much." [9]Then Jesus said to him, "Today salvation has come to this house." (Luke 19:5-9)

Zacchaeus' reaction to Jesus' unconditional love and acceptance was remarkable. Jesus had not accused him of fraud or told him he must give away his possessions. But Zacchaeus spontaneously responded as a changed man. Others that Jesus encountered responded in the same way. There truly is great power in unconditional love.

The most powerful manifestation of Jesus' unconditional love was demonstrated not in the way he lived but the manner in which he died. Evil people ridiculed, spit upon, whipped, and ultimately, crucified Jesus. What was his response to them? He forgave them! He prayed for those who crucified him, saying, "Father, forgive them; for they do not know what they are doing" (Luke 23:34). His forgiveness had a powerful, eye opening impact on many people, including the Roman centurion who was in charge of the crucifixion. After Jesus died, "when the centurion, who stood facing him, saw that in this way he breathed his last, he said, 'Truly this man was God's Son!'" (Mark 15:39).

Jesus forgave them all. What a power-packed expression of unconditional love! Jesus' enemies did not have the last word. The ways of Jesus prevailed. He achieved victory over sin, death, and the power of evil, not only for himself but also for all of humankind.

If Jesus had cursed those who crucified him, they would have felt justified in killing him. There would have been no power in his death. His death would have ended his influence. The Christian Church would never have come into existence. Jesus, however, did not curse his crucifiers, he loved them, prayed for them and forgave them. And as the saying goes, the rest is history. No one has influenced history as much as Jesus because of the very way he lived, and died. The power of Jesus' crucifixion has resulted in the conversion and transformation of billions of people over the centuries.

## Risk and Power in Following Jesus

Jesus calls us to follow his example and love others in a special way, to love them no matter what. I believe that is what he was talking about when he said, "If any want to become my followers, let them deny themselves and take up their cross daily and follow me" (Luke 9:23). It is a risky business to love others unconditionally, as Jesus taught us. Others may abuse and take advantage of us.

Let us not forget the example of Jesus in this regard. He too was abused and eventually killed. But he was not defeated. He achieved the ultimate victory. The same redemptive and transforming dynamics that enabled Jesus to exert a powerfully positive influence on many people are available to each of us in the way we might choose to treat each other.

In forgiving those who crucified him, Jesus also demonstrated for us that by forgiving others who have wronged us, we take away any power they may have over us. Tremendous powers for redemption and transformation results from our own undeserved suffering, while we continue to unconditionally love, accept and forgive those who impose the suffering.

The reason that to love and forgive those who inflict undeserved suffering upon us is so powerful is because it prevents defensiveness while it fosters repentance. If one strikes back at a perpetrator of injustice, a confrontation may likely ensue. But if one continues to love and forgive an aggressor, that love and forgiveness can result in self-examination by the guilty party. The feeling of guilt over the unjust infliction of pain upon you, an innocent person, leads that perpetrator to repent and to seek forgiveness. Often the result is a dramatic and positive internal change in that individual.

We may fear the prospect of how we might be treated if we give others the gift of unconditional love. It can be a crucifying experience. But just think of the continuous infusion of vitality and meaningfulness into our lives as we by God's grace and power daily take up such a cross and follow Jesus! Think of the lives of others that will be transformed! There is enormous power in living as a radical lover, like Jesus.

We do not have to do all things perfectly. When we demand perfection from ourselves it is inevitably self-defeating. But when we receive acceptance, support and encouragement at all times, we are empowered to go on to eventually exceed even our own greatest hopes, dreams and expectations, spiritually and in every other aspect of our lives. What power there is in loving and accepting someone else unconditionally! And what big benefits come from it!

Jesus said, "You shall love (agape) your neighbor as yourself" (Matthew 22:39). That tells us that to love others is possible if we love ourselves. We can carry this idea a step further and realize it is only when we love ourselves unconditionally that we are able to love others unconditionally as well. Self-love is wonderful and essential for a healthy, full, and happy life. How blessed we are when we learn to love ourselves unconditionally. We are then in a position to have a life-transforming influence on others after we learn to love them unconditionally as well.

## Putting Everything into God's Hands

I do not suggest that a person should passively let others abuse him or her, or that one should not protest or resist abuse, or that one should stay in a situation in which continued abuse is likely. What I do say is that, even in the most trying of circumstances, we need to continue to give unconditional love because in many situations, unconditional love, acceptance and forgiveness are the only forces powerful enough to penetrate the defenses and bring about transformation for a person desperately in need of help.

Unconditional love is an awesome power. But even it cannot always bring about immediate change. With all that we may do in our endeavor to love others and effect a positive influence upon them, they may not always respond as positively or quickly as we would like them to. Instead, they may shut our love out of their lives. When that happens, we need to continue to love them unconditionally anyway, and to put the whole situation into God's hands. In Melody Beattie's words, "We detach with the understanding that life is unfolding exactly as it needs to, for others and ourselves. . . . We do this with the understanding that a Power greater than ourselves is in charge and all is well."[1]

With this perspective we can be at peace, knowing that when the time is right, when the person is ready, by the grace of God he will be motivated and empowered to leave behind the darkness, cold and pain. He will begin to experience instead, the light, warmth and healing of life.

When we learn to love unconditionally, we will be able to stop acting judgmentally and critically of others. That is because we will interpret all of their responses to us, whether positive or negative, as falling into one of two categories; either as an expression of love or as an appeal for love. With this perspective, we will be enabled to love people in all circumstances.

How sad and tragic life would be without love. But, what beauty, majesty, fullness, and vitality our lives hold when we experience an abundance of love in it, especially unconditional love. There is enormous power in unconditional love - power to change lives - power to change the world - power to make every child feel special, loved and valuable - power to equip

every adult to live victoriously - power to eventually bring
every lost person home to be with God.


STUDY/DISCUSSION QUESTIONS:
1.  Can unconditional love and imposing everlasting
    punishment on people by God be compatible?
2.  Why is it that we all have such a deep need for love?
3.  Why was Jesus so quick to forgive?
4.  What was it that enabled Jesus to forgive his crucifiers?
5.  What are the risks and benefits of loving others
    unconditionally?
6.  How does it feel to be unconditionally loved?
7.  Why is self-love necessary in order to be able to love
    others?
8.  Why is there such power in unconditional love?
9.  How might we treat others differently if we considered
    everything they did as either an expression of love or an
    appeal for it?

# Lesson Nine

# FORGIVENESS IS ONLY THE BEGINNING

## Growing Into God's Likeness

It is not sufficient for the eternal well being of our spirits to merely receive forgiveness of our sins, as important as that is. Growth beyond forgiveness is absolutely essential for us as Christians if we are to ever experience heaven to its fullest. Forgiveness is not the end in itself. It is just the beginning of a new life. True, forgiveness is sufficient to help us begin to experience something of heaven and to be identified with God's people. But if we continue to live as sinners, our actions will naturally bring misery to ourselves and others, including our loved ones. People must be sincerely changed, transformed and healed - in other words, made whole, if heaven is going to be heavenly in the fullest sense for everyone.

Certainly, being healed and made whole emotionally and spiritually is at the heart of salvation. We need to affirm that if there is no healing in those respects there is ultimately no salvation. We must each be made into a new creation if we are ever going to be able to live together in such a way that all can experience heaven.

## Four Stages of Spiritual Growth

In trying to understand what it specifically means to grow spiritually, I have found noted psychologist and author, M. Scott Peck to be very helpful. In his book, *Further Along the Road Less Traveled*, he outlines four stages of spiritual growth. Following is a summary of those stages.[2]

People in stage one, *Chaotic/antisocial*, are characterized by an absence of spirituality and are unprincipled. Their lives are chaotic. In order to overcome the misery and chaos of their lives, some of them convert to stage two. In stage two, *Formal/institutional*, people depend upon the Church to govern their lives. The structure, dependability and predictability appeal to their need for stability, but God is viewed to be judgmental and to send some people to hell forever. Some people eventually begin to question the validity of the institutional church and certain teachings. At this point they have begun their conversion to spiritual stage three.

Those in stage three, *Skeptic/individual*, are not religious in the usual sense, but are more advanced spiritually than people in stage two. They are invariably truth seekers. As they seek truth, and the pieces of the larger picture start to come together, they are beginning their conversion to stage four. People in stage four, *Mystical/communal*, are able to see the interconnectedness between all of life and God. They are comfortable in a world of paradoxes and mystery, in contrast to those in stage two who are very uncomfortable when things are not clearly delineated.

I have observed that not everyone experiences each stage with the same intensity. Children of stage four parents often have a great advantage in growing through the spiritual stages. Some of their earliest memories are those of going to church. They cannot remember when God was not an important part of their lives. Like children of stage two parents, they internalize the teachings of the Church and become self-disciplined individuals. They, however, are able to avoid much of the rigidity and narrowness of stage two because they have always been encouraged to ask questions and be receptive to new thoughts. As a result, they are likely to experience little of the rebelliousness typically associated with the transition from stage two to three. As they mature, because their spiritual stage four parents have modeled its principles to them since early childhood, these people often move quite easily and naturally through stage three to four.

Many people do not begin the process of spiritual growth until they are adults. When that is the case, it is possible to move quickly through the spiritual stages. Sadly, however, many people become stuck in a stage and stop growing.

## Don't Get Stuck in a Lower Spiritual Stage

It is obviously in a person's best interest to grow beyond stage one. Unfortunately, some people are slow to make that transition. One obstacle that hinders them is what is perceived to be the negative side of stage two. While a person may be miserable in stage one, stage two may not seem to them to be much of an improvement. People tend to not want to associate with others they feel are judgmental or with a God whom they have been told may throw them into hell for an eternity. People in stage one generally have no knowledge of the liberating possibilities of stages three and four. That is because most churches as well as radio and television preachers focus only on the need to advance to stage two. In not realizing that there are opportunities for greater spiritual growth beyond stage two, some people choose to stay in stage one.

Then there are those who advance to stage two and stop growing, often without realizing that is the case. I have known many people who are stuck in stage two, even while they emphasize the importance of growth. They believe that they are growing spiritually, but their growth all takes place within stage two. They are terrified by the possibility that they may have doubts and questions. This to them suggests a lack of faith or commitment on their part. They will not let themselves entertain a skeptical thought. They allow themselves only to think and do what they have been taught to think and do. They find security in pat answers. They need things to be spelled out in very clear terms. Without realizing it, these people are in a rut. Growth for them does not involve expanding the rut but only in digging it deeper. If people at that place in their spiritual development are ever going to move on to stages three and four, they are going to have to muster the courage to peek out over the sides of their rut and begin to explore the broader world.

A person staying within the confines of stage two is like a butterfly remaining inside its cocoon. Living in a cocoon does not require much thinking. Life is predictable. The safety and security of a closed world is very appealing to some people. The broader world is beyond their comprehension or appreciation and can be mysterious and frightening to them. They do not realize there are legitimate beliefs beyond their way of thinking. They naively believe that their little world is all that exists, or that at least there is nothing of ultimate truth or importance beyond their realm. Sadly, they do not have an appreciation of the fact that there is a whole new world out there that is enjoyed by liberated butterflies.

Some churches want their members to stay in cocoons. They are easier to keep in line. Cocooned parishioners do not ask difficult questions, and they do not venture out on their own. Butterflies, on the other hand, explore freely. Their lives are exciting, fun and rewarding, though uncontrollable and somewhat risky. There is no end to the possibilities in a butterfly's unfettered world for learning and growth.

Jesus used the analogy of wind to describe his followers, those who are born of the Spirit. He said, "The wind blows where it chooses, and you hear the sound of it, but you do not know where it comes from or where it goes" (John 3:8). The wind is unpredictable and beyond our control. Jesus goes on to say, "So it is with everyone who is born of the Spirit" (John 3:8).

Sadly, not only do many people in spiritual stage two fail to grow beyond that stage themselves, but worse, they prevent others from moving on as well. This is not a new phenomenon. Jesus observed it in the scribes and Pharisees, the most staunch stage two people of his day. He told them, "But woe to you scribes, Pharisees, hypocrites! For you lock people out of the kingdom of heaven. For you do not go in yourselves, and when others are going in, you stop them" (Matthew 23:13).

Stage two people often feel threatened and concerned when they witness others moving into stage three, which they see manifested in the expression of honest questions and doubts. Their deep concerns are based on the misinterpretation of where the people growing into stage three are headed. It appears that the others are not progressing spiritually, but have slid back to spiritual stage one. They mistakenly believe that those who are growing have actually lost their faith and abandoned Christ. This conclusion is inevitable for them because, while they are familiar with stages one and two, they have no first hand knowledge of stages three and four. They have not experienced them. Indeed, they are not aware that there are possibilities for growth beyond their present spiritual level. For them, stage two is the model for Christianity and the ultimate standard for the faith. They cannot comprehend how anyone with questions and doubts could be more advanced spiritually than they.

When people grow from stage two to three, often interpreted as backsliding, the immediate response of those remaining in stage two is to try to lasso the people they believe have gone astray and lead them back into the fold. To use another analogy, stage two people often chase after newly liberated butterflies with a net in an attempt to bring them back into the cocoon. Though well intentioned, the end result of these efforts is that they hinder others from progressing into stage three. Without realizing it, they are holding others back in their spiritual growth. Sadly, they prevent many people from ever reaching the ultimate spiritual experience of stage four.

While it is unfortunate to get stuck in stage two, it is not necessarily better to move on to stage three and stop there. Remaining plagued by unresolved questions and doubts is neither enriching nor fulfilling. There is no power in a life of uncertainty.

In light of the above, you can see our goal should be to move through the spiritual stages to stage four. Vitality, power and excitement become realities when our inner confusion and questions are resolved, when spiritual truths come into focus and are ingrained in our lives.

## Growth for Eternity

I believe growth is as essential in the next life as it is in our earthly existence; it is just not possible to do all of our growing here. Each of us uses only a small percentage of the mental capacity given us. We are far from developing our full physical potential as well, a fact born out by the many people who continue to set new world records in athletic competition. When I think of the possibilities of depth in our spiritual growth, it is apparent to me that most of us have only begun to grow.

In the Christian faith we celebrate the present reality as well as future expectation. It is wonderful to experience joy, peace, forgiveness, empowerment, love, and so much more. Yet, looking to the future, we can expect fulfillment and happiness far beyond what we can even imagine now. I can hardly wait for what tomorrow will bring.

Growth is necessary, and is possible throughout eternity. It is possible because of the power, love and grace of God. Because God is great, wonderful and powerful, there is no limit to the possibilities for growth. Our ultimate goal is to become as one with God.

Those who die and go to heaven will not have arrived at their final destination. No one will ever arrive, nor should it necessarily be considered desirable to do so. To have arrived could be like retiring, our work done, with nothing left to do; no more challenges, or learning, or growth. If that is the case, to have arrived could make heaven seem boring and unfulfilling. If it were ever truly possible to have arrived, would not that also open up the possibility of pride and smugness on the part of those who thought they had arrived (which would only prove that they had not)? Heaven would not be completely heavenly if that were possible.

Unending growth naturally implies that we will not only need the grace and forgiveness of God at this time, in this life, but we always will. In our journey as imperfect people who have not arrived, in this life and the next, God helps us to grow, nurtures us along, and forgives our failures and shortcomings all along the way.

One way to express this is to say that God functions as our counselor, now as well as later. The understanding of God as our counselor should come as no surprise to us since the Messiah is referred to as, "Wonderful Counselor, Mighty God" (Isaiah 9:6). In reference to the Holy Spirit, Jesus said that the Father "will give you another Advocate (commonly translated Counselor), to be with you forever" (John 14:16).

Many of us are too proud to willingly seek out a counselor. But if we could get beyond our pride, we might discover the purpose of such a relationship; to help us gain insight into our behavior and ourselves. A counselor is one who holds us accountable for our actions, one that helps us overcome our misconceptions and leads us in a path of growth. Through such a process we might learn to let go of our addictions, fears, prejudices and our need to control others. We might learn to be loving, forgiving, kind, healthy and whole. God's Spirit is our greatest counselor now, along with truly spiritual and insightful people who help guide us in God's ways. I believe that through the Holy Spirit and those gifted individuals God provides, our growth process will continue into eternity.

Heaven offers the possibility, indeed, the necessity of continual, eternal growth as one advances toward the fullness of God. I believe that is what Paul is referring to in 2 Corinthians 12:2, where he writes, "I know a person in Christ who fourteen years ago was caught up in the third heaven." This Scripture suggests there are different levels which one may experience in one's relationship with God and others in heaven, where people "with unveiled faces, seeing the glory of the Lord. . . . are being transformed into the same image from one degree of glory to another" (2 Corinthians 3:18).

STUDY/DISCUSSION QUESTIONS:

1. How close do any of us come to reaching our full potential, mentally, physically and spiritually in this life?
2. How do the four stages of spiritual growth relate to you?
3. Do you know people in each of the four spiritual stages?
4. Why do the majority of churchgoers fit in stage two?
5. How is it that, even with the questions and doubts of the people in stage three, they are still more advanced spiritually than those in stage two?
6. What stage were your parents in when you were growing up, and how did that affect you?
7. What concerns you most about the negative aspects of spiritual stages one, two and three?
8. Do you understand how and why people in churches can sometimes hinder others from growing spiritually?
9. How are you striving to be a butterfly?
10. In what ways do you expect to continue to grow, in this life and the next?

# Lesson Ten

# MISERY LOVES COMPANY

## Why Some People Cling to the Idea
## of Eternal Damnation

God will eventually save everyone. What a thought! What a resounding acclamation! Sadly, though, many people do not believe in it, so they cannot join in the joyful celebration. We cannot blame most of them because they have never been told about universal salvation. When they are told, many respond favorably while others are somewhat cautious about accepting the news. Some people, upon hearing of universal salvation, consider it such good news that they latch onto it like a child onto a teddy bear.

### Negative Responses to the Good News
In bold contrast to the joyous enthusiasm of many people, others seem determined not to believe that everyone will be saved. It amazes me how some folks cling so tenaciously to the very unpleasant concept of eternal damnation, rather than to embrace the good news of universal salvation. An announcement that God will eventually save everyone should cause great relief, celebration and dancing in the streets. You would think people (especially Christians, who claim to serve a God of love and compassion) would welcome the idea that no

one will have to spend eternity in hell. But that is not always the case.

Why is it that the teaching of eternal damnation is so near and dear to the hearts of some people that they are not about to give it up under any circumstance? After wrestling with that question, I have come to realize the first clue is that it is near and dear to their hearts. It is not that the idea of eternal damnation is so special, but that their personal beliefs are fastened to their hearts like the love reserved for the closest of friends. They have received great comfort and security in what they have believed, perhaps for many decades. Changing beliefs after that length of time is like closing the door on their oldest companions.

Also, many people are threatened by change. It is frightening to follow truth wherever it leads. Some people are unable or unwilling to attempt it; in their insecurities they cling to the past, to what is familiar, to what seems safe.

We can understand why many people will not accept the hope of universalism, but those factors do not explain why some react so strongly against it. Some people become judgmental or downright hostile toward me when I tell them that God will eventually save everyone. I struggled to understand why they reacted that way, until some of the reasons were verbalized to me, and then other more subtle reasons slowly became apparent.

## Verbalized Reasons for Opposing Universalism

The most common reason people have given me for rejecting universalism is that they do not believe the Bible supports it. They have often heard the passages that seem to support unending punishment of the unsaved but they have rarely heard any of the ones that support universal salvation. This is complicated by the fact that Bible passages are often interpreted in several different ways. When I have spoken to them of the often overlooked and misunderstood passages, they may initially feel unnerved or threatened. They believe I am tampering with the Scriptures. This strikes at the very foundation of their faith and the religion they believe they should never question. The most strongly expressed motivation for those who oppose universal salvation is fear. They fear that if the fact that God will eventually save everyone becomes widely known, some people (especially their own children or other loved ones) will not take hell seriously. As a result, some of their precious loved ones may be inclined to live in an evil way while they still expect to get into heaven. What if they enter the next life only to learn it does not work that way? With that thought in mind, some people, out of genuine concern for the eternal well-being of their loved ones, emphatically reject the idea that God will eventually save everyone. Consequently, they sometimes emotionally berate those who believe God will.

## Co-dependence

I believe there often exists an unhealthy co-dependent relationship between the Church and its members. That, unfortunately, gives people a psychological reason to cling to the belief in eternal damnation. Co-dependence involves an unhealthy perception of oneself and relating to other people in detrimental ways. There are many characteristics of co-dependency, including; an inability to deal with feelings openly, the need to maintain control over others and situations, the inordinate need to please others, perfectionism, dishonesty, fearfulness, rigidity, judgmentalism, self-centeredness, and negativism.

Leaders in the field of co-dependency contend that the majority of people are co-dependent to one degree or another. Many factors contribute to this, including the dynamics of relationships in our families, schools, places of employment, and even churches. Co-dependency is pervasive throughout our culture and has a major effect on people's lives, yet many people fail to recognize it.

While we prefer to believe that the Church has only a positive influence on people's lives, I am saddened to realize that is not always the case. The Church sometimes contributes to this problem of co-dependency by way of an unhealthy use of power and control. As special as the Church is, it is not without blemish or weakness. One weakness is co-dependency. The co-dependent relationship that often exists between the Church and its members is a significant reason for the perpetuation of the teaching of eternal damnation. Conversely, teaching eternal damnation perpetuates co-dependency. It is a vicious cycle.

## Co-dependence Throughout Church History

To understand the cycle of co-dependency within churches, it is helpful to put it into a historical perspective. To a large degree this revolves around the theologian and Church leader Augustine and his teachings. Universal salvation was well accepted and widely believed by Christians until the sixth century. It was then banished due to the influence of Augustine's teachings against it. Thereafter, the teaching of everlasting punishment of the unsaved prevailed in the Church for over 1,000 years.

The teaching of eternal damnation gave the Church tremendous power and control over its members through the threat of excommunication, which amounted to being expelled from the Church. The teeth in this threat was the perception that the Church was the exclusive dispenser of salvation, and that the Church held the keys to heaven and hell. In those days, if a worshipper was expelled from the Church, it was believed that he or she had been given a one-way ticket to hell. With the understanding that a person who went to hell would be confined there forever, church members did not take the Church's mandates lightly.

Another way the Church controlled its members was to keep them ignorant of the Scriptures by copying the Bible only in Latin. Virtually no one but priests learned Latin, so the common people were completely at the mercy of the priests and church leaders. The priests told the people only what they wanted them to know, which included eternal damnation for the unsaved, but nothing about universalism. The common people were taught the "party line" and threatened with eternal damnation if they did not follow it. As you can see, in the Church, there existed a very unhealthy co-dependent relationship. The Church exercised total control over its members, while the members allowed themselves to be controlled. They often did not think for themselves, but instead, did what they were told to do in exchange for the promise of salvation.

This extreme situation continued until the time of the Protestant Reformation, which began under the leadership of Martin Luther in the year 1517. With the formation of other churches, the threat of excommunication was no longer as dire a circumstance because, if expelled, a person could join another church. That, however, would have been like jumping out of the frying pan into the fire. All churches taught the eternal damnation of the unsaved. None were willing to give up that foolproof way to control their members. Also, collectively, the churches of the day still considered themselves the exclusive conduit of salvation.

The invention of the printing press was probably the most significant development that made the Protestant Reformation possible. Because of its use, Bibles and other literature in the languages of the people could be produced in large quantities. People no longer had to simply accept the teachings of those few who could read and interpret Bibles written in Latin. Consequently, the Church could no longer control the people by keeping them ignorant of what the Scriptures really taught.

Even after personal Bibles were made available, however, ministers and church leaders still told the people what to consider as the correct interpretation of the Bible. This so called correct interpretation did not include the teaching of salvation for everyone, but emphasized eternal damnation of the unsaved. The clergy and church leaders, eager to hang on to their means of controlling people, instilled in them fear of eternal damnation. In their conspiracy of silence regarding universal salvation, it seems they hoped no one would discover the passages of Scripture that support it. But that was not possible. People began to read the Bible and to think for themselves. They discovered those overlooked and misunderstood passages and some of them started to believe, like so many Christians in the early Church, that God will eventually save everyone. By the eighteenth century, universalism once again became a strong movement; many people came to believe in it. Still they very rarely received any official endorsement of their belief by the churches.

## Co-dependence Today

Co-dependence remains a powerful force in some churches. Many people are still told, to a lesser or greater extent, what they must believe. Nearly all churches continue to uphold the belief in the eternal punishment in hell of the unsaved. There is a resounding silence emanating from seminaries and from churches with regard to the question of universal salvation. Apparently the Church still hopes that people will not discover this concept of hope on their own. Also, many Christians consider the organized Church as the official and exclusive dispenser of salvation.

In order to be fair to the many different denominations and individual churches, I need to make it clear that there are many differences between churches. In churches that have a low level of co-dependence, people are not taught a rigid set of beliefs, but are encouraged to think for themselves. Fear is not used as a means to control. The benefits of serving God are emphasized rather than the consequences of an unfaithful life. God is usually portrayed as loving and forgiving, not angry and judgmental.

In contrast to the churches with low co-dependency, there are others with very high levels. They can be identified by their insistence that all of their members adhere to certain specific beliefs. Thinking for oneself is strongly discouraged. Hell-fire and brimstone sermons are common. A strong sense of urgency is pressed upon the members to get themselves saved before they die. They not only teach that the Church in general is indispensable, but often contend that their specific church is the only true way to God and heaven.

Lesson Nine outlined the four stages of spiritual growth, and it is my belief that most churchgoers are in stage two of their spiritual development. They are those who fit quite comfortably into the co-dependent relationship that exists between the Church and its members. They look to the Church for structure, governance (control), and guidance on how to live their lives. While they believe that God is a loving being, they tend to think of God as one who does not hesitate to punish sinners.

We also should not be surprised to discover that people experiencing stage two in their spiritual development are those who get the most upset with and judgmental of others who espouse the teaching of universal salvation. The tenets of universalism strike at much of what has become sacred and dear to them, and it exposes their co-dependence. That is a frightening discovery. The more co-dependent a person is, the more he or she is threatened by the concept of universal salvation.

Co-dependency within the Church is a very enticing trap. In its most extreme form, the gains for the leaders and for the Church in general are obvious; the power, control, and authority over members who give generous donations while they volunteer their time to keep the Church operating. What the members get out of this arrangement is the promise of salvation.

There is also another dimension to what the members receive. As saved members of the Church, and a part of the in-group, they can feel something of that same sense of power and control that is exerted over them. As a result, they often make pronouncements regarding who is saved or lost. They perceive that they speak on behalf of God.

Sadly, this co-dependent relationship is not likely to end soon, nor is the teaching of eternal damnation. These two factors are bound together and perpetuate one another. Without the teaching of eternal damnation, the Church would lose its ability to manipulate and control. When we believe that God will eventually save everyone, including saving people from hell, we are forced to realize and admit that we do not have control. God does! Isn't it just like God to be out of control (Out of our control, that is)? Many people tend to not like a God such as that. They prefer to believe that they are in control.

Before leaving this subject, I need to state that dependence in relationships is not bad in and of itself. Far from it! It can be very healthy to depend on others in various ways. Children depend on their parents for guidance as well as to satisfy their many physical and emotional needs. We all depend on friends and loved ones for support, encouragement and help. Mutually dependent and supportive relationships help us to learn and grow, to enable us to relate to God and others in such a way that we experience heaven in this life and beyond. Ultimately, we depend upon God for salvation, who by grace gives it to us as a free gift. Dependence can be, and often is, wonderfully positive. It is important that the Church be about nurturing those kinds of positive relationships.

Sadly, however, we need to be aware that dependence in relationships sometimes slips into co-dependence, which can be very destructive. Instead of encouragement, there is control. Instead of hope, there is fear. Instead of support, there is judgment. Instead of forgiveness, there is the expectation of perfection. Instead of openness, there is dishonesty. Co-dependence can produce profoundly negative consequences in the way people relate to each other, including in the Church.

God, heal us of our co-dependence and make us whole. Amen!

STUDY/DISCUSSION QUESTIONS:
1.  Why aren't all Christians able to celebrate the good news of salvation for everyone?
2.  Why is considering change in our beliefs so threatening?
3.  Do you fear that some may not take hell seriously if they are told that everyone will eventually be saved?
4.  What causes co-dependence?

5. Why do some people feel such a need to control others? And why are others so receptive to being controlled?
6. What would be the benefits if seminaries taught universal salvation?
7. What is the level of co-dependence in your church?
8. Why are many people comfortable with a co-dependent relationship between themselves and their church?
9. How does not being able to control God make you feel?
10. How can we foster healthy dependent relationships with other people and God?

# Lesson Eleven

# THE ANCIENTS HAVE STOLEN OUR BEST IDEAS

## The History Of Universalism

### The Early Church

It was widely believed in the early centuries of the Christian Church that God would eventually save everyone. In contrast, the doctrine of endless punishment in hell for the unsaved was widely believed by pagans and heathens before the time of Christ and into the early years of the Church. The Jews also believed it. When people of those religions were converted to Christianity they sometimes retained their belief of unending punishment of the wicked. During the time of the early Church, some Christians believed the unsaved would merely be annihilated. Others believed in endless punishment in the hereafter. Still others taught that God would eventually save everyone.[1]

The first Christian theological school was founded in Alexandria in the second century. Clement and Origen, who were leading teachers at that school, believed very strongly that God would eventually save everyone. Origen, who was born of Christian parents in 186 A.D.,[2] wrote in his book, *On First Principles*, "There is a resurrection of the dead, and there is punishment but not everlasting. For when the body is punished the soul is gradually purified."[3] During that time, universal salvation was taught not only in Alexandria, but in three other schools as well; at Caesarea, Antioch and Edessa.[4]

There are many indications that universal salvation was widely accepted in the early Church. It was commonly taught that Christ had preached the Gospel to the dead in Hades, and many contended that all of the damned were released. Prayers for the release of the dead from hell were very common, which would have been foolishness if people believed that their fate had been irretrievably fixed at the time of death.[5] Works refuting all the known heresies of the times were written by Irenaeus (120-202 A.D.) and Hippolytus (170-235 A.D.). Universalism was not listed among them.[6]

Universalism was still a very strong belief in the fourth century,[7] when the theologian and bishop, Gregory of Nyssa (c. 335-394)[8] forcefully taught that God would eventually save everyone. Aside from Augustine, the two most influential people in the Church during the second half of the fourth century were Ambrose and Jerome.[9] They both believed in universal salvation.

## Augustine

Augustine's (354-430 A.D.) father was a heathen and his mother, a Christian. Augustine was converted to Christianity at the age of 32.[10] Consistent with his heathen roots, Augustine believed in the endless punishment of the wicked. He strongly challenged those who believed that everyone would be saved. He wrote, "Now I must. . .deal. . .with some of our own tenderhearted fellow Christians, who are inclined to feel that there must sooner or later be liberation from hell. . .that happiness will be eternal for all who, sooner or later, are freed from torments. . . . But the fact is that the more merciful the theory is, the more it contradicts the words of God and, therefore, the further it is from the truth."[11] The fact that Augustine addressed the issue of universalism and spoke so forcefully against it is an indication of how strong the movement was then.

## Opposition and Condemnation of Universalism

Augustine, who was a great theologian in many respects, developed a significant following and his theology soon became dominant in the Church. Largely due to his influence, there came to be increasing opposition to the doctrine of universal salvation.

The Emperor Justinian ruled the Roman Empire from 527 to 565 A.D. During his reign, church leaders who opposed Origen's teachings sought his help and support in stopping the spread of the belief that God would eventually save everyone. In 543 Justinian issued an Imperial Edict in which he attacked Origen and his teachings, including those regarding the limited duration of all punishment.[12] Justinian convened the Fifth Ecumenical Council at Constantinople in the spring of 553. That Council issued 15 statements condemning the teachings of Origen.[13] After that condemnation of Origenist Theology, some of Origen's teachings, including his position on universal salvation, were considered heresy throughout the Church.

To make his edict effective, Justinian went so far as to order that thereafter no bishop or abbot should be ordained unless he condemned universalism. Any bishop or abbot who refused to do so was to be deposed and banished. Following Justinian's edict, the belief in universalism was of necessity kept secret by its adherents. With all the forces of the Church and State against it, the teaching that God will eventually save everyone naturally declined in popularity. After a period of time it virtually died out.[14]

Does it seem strange to you that the Roman Emperor, Justinian, became so involved in the concerns of the Church? This will make complete sense when you see it in the context of co-dependence, where the control of others and situations is a major dynamic. By the sixth century the Roman emperor exerted a great deal of influence over the Church. That was a dramatic change when compared to the situation prior to the early part of the fourth century. At that time, Emperor Constantine declared Christianity an officially accepted and favored religion of the empire. Before Constantine had granted that supposed favor, the Church was a completely independent entity and did not support the State. After Constantine's declaration, a co-dependent relationship quickly developed between the Church and the State. In exchange for acceptance and the elimination of persecution, the Church allowed the State to have a significant amount of influence and control over it. Also, the Church began the practice of giving largely unquestioned support of the State and its conquests and policies.

Before the fourth century most Christians were pacifists who refused to serve in the emperor's armed forces. After Constantine's acceptance of Christianity, Christians began to waiver from their pacifist principles. Rather than to love their enemies as Jesus commanded them according to Matthew 5:43-44, they began to rationalize that it was all right to kill. Once they had convinced themselves it was acceptable to God to hate and destroy enemies, it was a short step for many of them to also believe that God would punish sinners forever. Conversely, those who already believed in unending punishment, with the corresponding violent perception of God, had few serious qualms about serving in the emperor's army.

After more than 200 years of the militarization of the Church and its related eroding effects on Universalist teachings, Justinian became the emperor. Justinian was motivated more by politics than by religious convictions. When the controversy over universal salvation arose it was natural for him to side with those who opposed universalism. They were the ones who were most supportive of him, and the ones he could most easily control. The free spirited Universalists were not easily controlled and thus were considered a threat to others in the Church as well as to the emperor.

It is not surprising; therefore, that Justinian and those who opposed universalism joined forces. They outlawed Universalist teachings and reinforced the doctrine of eternal damnation as a means of attempting to bring everyone under control. This also had the effect of perpetuating the co-dependent relationship between the Church and the State.

## John Wesley

The doctrine of universal salvation lay largely dormant for several centuries. Eventually it started to revive, and became quite strong again by the eighteenth century. That was when John Wesley (1703-1791) came on the scene. He was one of the founders of the Methodist movement and had a close association with the Moravians, a body of dedicated Christians who believed in universal salvation. They had a significant influence on him. From early in his ministry, Wesley's teachings held much in common with those who taught that God would eventually save everyone, though during the early part of his ministry he did not embrace universalism.

Later in his life, however, Wesley's beliefs had evolved to the point where he endorsed universalism. That is illustrated by a sermon that he preached on March 13, 1782, entitled, "On The Fall of Man," in which he said that God loves everyone and God's mercy extends to all. He further contended that God, who alone is able to do it, has provided a remedy for all the evils of humankind. The sufficient remedy for all our guilt is that Christ bore all our sins on the cross. God in his mercy has provided "an universal remedy for an universal evil! In appointing the Second Adam to die for all who had died in the first: that 'as in Adam all died, so in Christ all might be made alive;' that 'as by one man's offense judgment came upon all men to condemnation, so by the righteousness of one' the free gift 'might come upon all, unto justification of life.'"[15]

## The American Colonies

The American colonies proved to be the most fertile ground for the spread of the teaching of universalism in the eighteenth century. Dr. George DeBenneville, of French Huguenot background, migrated to Pennsylvania in 1741. He was instrumental in the spreading of Universalist views. John Murray (1741-1815), though, who came from England in 1770, is considered the father of organized Universalism.[16]

While Murray was very actively involved in church work in England, he did not preach on a regular basis until after he came to America. Upon his arrival, Murray was befriended by both Quaker and German Baptists who openly taught universalism.[17] With their encouragement he began to preach regularly,[18] and he had significant success in spreading universalism even though there was much opposition.[19] The Universalists, under Murray's leadership, organized their own church on January 1, 1779.[20]

Hosea Ballou (1771-1852) was a dominant figure in the Universalist Church during his lifetime. By the time he died in 1852 there was more than 800,000 adherents to the universalist faith.[21] The Universalist Church of America merged with the American Unitarian Association in 1961 to become the Unitarian Universalist Association.[22]

## Dietrich Bonhoeffer

Dietrich Bonhoeffer (German theologian and church leader who was put to death in a concentration camp during World War II because of his opposition to the Nazis) believed that the central message of the New Testament is that God reconciled the world with Godself through Christ. He wrote that "the world is not divided between Christ and the devil, but whether it recognizes it or not, it is solely and entirely the world of Christ. . . . There is no part of the world, be it never so forlorn and never so godless, which is not accepted by God and reconciled with God in Jesus Christ."[23]

## Karl Barth

Renowned twentieth century Swiss theologian, Karl Barth wrote, "The witness of the community of God to every individual man consists in this: that this choice (rejecting God) of the godless man is void; that he belongs eternally to Jesus Christ and therefore is not rejected, but elected by God in Jesus Christ; that the rejection which he deserves on account of his perverse choice is borne and cancelled by Jesus Christ; that he is appointed to eternal life with God on the basis of the righteous, divine decision."[24]

## Paul Tillich

In answer to the question, "who shall be saved, liberated, healed?" the German-born twentieth century American theologian, Paul Tillich writes, "The fourth gospel says: the world! The reunion with the eternal from which we come, from which we are separated, to which we shall return, is promised to everything that is."[25]

## A Long Rich History

As we can clearly see, the belief in universal salvation is not a recent development. It is not a modern liberal idea, as some might suggest. Universalism has a long rich history. Christians throughout much of the history of the Church have advocated it, especially during the first six centuries and in the last three. The proponents have not always agreed on all points, such as whether or not there will even be hell in the next life, but millions of Christians over time have strongly believed and enthusiastically celebrated that God will eventually save everyone.

STUDY/DISCUSSION QUESTIONS:
1. How are your beliefs about salvation affected by knowing that universal salvation was widely believed by the early Christians?
2. How might history have been different if Augustine had never lived?
3. What are the implications of Justinian entering the fight against the Universalists?
4. In what ways is there a co-dependent relationship between the Church and State today?
5. What made the American colonies so receptive to the message of universal salvation?
6. Why is it that so many leading theologians have believed in universalism, yet their beliefs have not become widely known?
7. How might the comeback of universalism give you hope?

# Lesson  Twelve

# MAKING MOUNTAINS OUT OF MOUNTAINS

## The Significance of This Issue

The eternal hell idea is not merely a harmless untruth, about which we can appropriately keep quiet. We may be tempted to not oppose it to avoid the risk of rejection or condemnation from others. But we must speak out against it. Neither is universal salvation an idea we should keep to ourselves. The importance of sharing the good news of salvation for everyone cannot be overstated. The doctrine of hell has had such an exaggerated place in theology and preaching for so long that for many Christians the good news of the gospel has been overshadowed by the bad news about judgment and punishment. This has gone on far too long, and with devastating consequences.

### Atheism

The belief that God sends people to unending hell causes many people to turn away from God. The reason for this is expressed very well by Samuel Clemens (AKA Mark Twain), where he writes of

> a God who could make good children as easily as bad,
> yet preferred to make bad ones; who could have made

every one of them happy, yet never made a single happy one; who made them prize their bitter life, yet stingily cut it short; who gave his angels eternal happiness unearned, yet required his other children to earn it; who gave his angels painless lives, yet cursed his other children with biting miseries and maladies of mind and body; who mouths justice and invented hell - mouths mercy and invented hell - mouths Golden Rules, and forgiveness multiplied by seventy times seven, and invented hell; who mouths morals to other people and has none himself; who frowns upon crimes, yet commits them all; who created man without invitation, then tries to shuffle the responsibility for man's acts upon man, instead of honorably placing it where it belongs, upon himself; and finally, with altogether divine obtuseness, invites this poor, abused slave to worship him![1]

Not everyone is able to express this as articulately as Twain, but many people feel that way. And they reject God. A strong case can be made that a major reason for atheism is the teaching of a God of eternal damnation.

Mark Twain was the victim of the teaching of eternal damnation. He could not accept the idea of everlasting punishment. Sadly, he threw the baby out with the dirty bath water. He rejected God as well. That caused him to experience a hell of meaninglessness. Countless others have rejected God for the same reason, and with similar results.

## Communism

According to Robert Short, the development of modern Fascism and Communism was inevitable because of the teaching of endless punishment in hell.[2] Ponder for a moment the implications of this. It is tragic when one person becomes an atheist. It is a tragedy of monumental proportions when atheism becomes institutionalized, as has been the case in the countries of the Soviet Union, China, Cuba and others. While I know that there are many complex reasons for what happens within nations, I believe those countries would have been much less likely to become officially atheistic if God had been consistently presented in a more favorable and accurate way.

Now, Communism is crumbling, which is inevitable with atheism, and the Church is leading the way in overcoming it. But this time, may the Church abandon its teachings on the God of eternal damnation and thus prevent a resurgence of atheism in the future.

## Satanism

Certainly one of the most significant and tragic consequences of the teaching of eternal damnation is the rise of Satanism. It's clear from their teachings that they have rejected God and Christianity because of the teaching of eternal damnation.

In the end, Satanists "tell themselves 'This is for me-- why should I continue with a religion which condemns me for everything I do, even though there is nothing actually wrong with it?'"[3] And they declare, "We are no longer supplicating weaklings trembling before an unmerciful 'God' who cares not whether we live or die. We are self-respecting, prideful people--we are Satanists!"[4]

## Lukewarm Christianity

A major concern in all churches is inactive members or lukewarm Christians. Teaching of a God of eternal damnation contributes to this situation. A schizophrenic God, who supposedly has great love for people but never the less sends many of them to unending hell, can never have very much success in influencing people. It seems to me that many people are drawn to the Church and stay in church for the purpose of getting saved, but they cannot bring themselves to be very enthusiastic about serving such a God.

## The Unchurched

Perhaps half of the population does not go to church, even on Christmas or Easter. I have found that unchurched people so often bring up the subject of hell it is obvious to me that the teaching that God will punish people in hell forever is an issue that weighs heavily upon them. It is as if they feel a strong need to make a rebuttal against what they have often heard about the God of eternal damnation. They hope someone will agree with them, and tell them it is not so, that God really is not like that. They seem to instinctively know God would not throw some people into hell and leave them there for eternity. Consequently, they reject the idea of hell, and sometimes they reject God as well. At that point, they are definitely not really interested in going to church. They cannot bring themselves to worship with those who believe in a God of eternal damnation.

We deny our members power and enthusiasm because we continue teaching eternal damnation. People sense that while the church claims to have good news, they do not find it to be particularly newsworthy. The truly Good News of the gospel is that Jesus suffered and died to save everyone. That is the kind of news we can get excited about!

## Making the World a Better Place

We all want to make the world a better place, but that is not likely to become a reality as long as we continue to teach that God imposes or enforces endless punishment in hell. The perception of a cruel God produces cruel Christians. As Short says, "People always tend to resemble the gods they serve. A vindictive God always produces vindictiveness among those he influences."[5]

People are not necessarily more humane in the way they treat others because they belong to a church. The self-righteous often pass judgment, handily aided by the Bible. If we believe that God is sometimes vengeful, judgmental, unforgiving, and uncaring, it is easy for us to justify exhibiting at times those same characteristics ourselves. On the other hand, if we really believe that God never condones ungodly behavior and are convinced that God is consistently loving, kind and forgiving, we are more likely to always act that way ourselves.

The world can become a much better place when we

change our understanding of hell and God. God is not vengeful, but is always loving of everyone. When we really understand that, and fully assimilate it into our minds and hearts, we can then appreciate the preciousness of others. It is in the example of Christ that we find the basis for loving all humans as they really are. We love each other, not because anyone is perfect, but because we learn to love as God loves. When we realize that God loves us in our imperfections, we also can learn to love unconditionally.

Unfortunately, it is true that when we emphasize the existence of hell with the same force as we do the existence of heaven, there are those of us who are all too ready to populate hell with those deemed unworthy of heaven. After we condemn the obvious ones such as Judas, Hitler and terrorists, why not go on to others that some may find reprehensible? The list could be endless.

Persisting in the belief that some folks go to heaven and others go to hell for eternity sometimes results in those who suppose they are saved becoming very judgmental of those whom they perceive to be lost. With self-righteous indignation they may look down on those whom they think did not have the good sense to accept Christ as their Savior. They may also be very critical of those who have a somewhat different understanding of the faith than they do.

That kind of a judgmental attitude does not foster goodwill and brotherhood. Instead, it can cause a person to feel justified in committing all kinds of atrocities. Tragically, over the centuries, some of the most devoutly religious people have been guilty of perpetrating (or at least defending) blatantly unchristian actions, such as; the crucifixion of Jesus, the Inquisition (through which many thousands of "heretics" were killed), other bitter religious persecutions, and numerous wars.

In believing, on the other hand, that Christ has provided salvation for all and that God will ultimately take everyone to heaven, we can view others from a new perspective. We can no longer justify being judgmental, condemning and cruel to others. We will instead feel inclined to relate to everyone else as redeemed children of God, people who are to be respected, considered precious, and treated as one's brothers and sisters.

## Loving Our Enemies

With that attitude, our love can extend even to our enemies. We can love our enemies, because God does. We can have unity with our enemies not only because we all have God as our parent, but also because of our common evil. When we are able to acknowledge our own inner shadow, we will naturally become more tolerant of the shadow in others. In other words, when we learn to love the enemy within, we can develop the compassion and understanding we need to love the enemy without.

The good news is that God is not hostile, toward our enemies or us. We are all in the same situation, friends and enemies alike, all accepted and loved by God, all redeemed by God's grace. We are one in our evil and one in our redemption. All of us are brothers and sisters, children of a loving parent. Thanks be to God!

## Bad News Versus Good News

It is amazing to me that the teaching of universal salvation is perceived by some people to be bad news. They emphatically reject it. But it is good news! In fact, it is the best possible news. How could anything be better? Universal salvation is something to accept and celebrate with unbridled enthusiasm.

## Jesus Said, "Let Your Light Shine"

We have good news!!! It is the promise of salvation for everyone. Because it is such good news and is so important, we need to be about the business of sharing it. Let us boldly tell it; to our children, parents, relatives, co-workers, neighbors, friends, enemies, to everyone around the world. It is not only our responsibility but also a high privilege to spread the Good News. We read in 2 Corinthians 5:19; "In Christ God was reconciling the world to himself, not counting their trespasses against them, and entrusting the message of reconciliation to us."

If we who believe in universal salvation keep quiet instead of speaking up, the only message that people will hear is the untrue and incredibly bad news of eternal damnation. We must not be intimidated into silence, but freely spread the Good News. Salvation is complete. Karl Barth says, "The task of the church is to announce the good news of the perfect work of Christ done for all. . . . The distinction is not between redeemed and non-redeemed, but between those who realize it and those who do not."[6]

May we help others realize and experience the salvation that Christ has provided for all of us.

STUDY/DISCUSSION QUESTIONS:

1.  What results are likely if we keep the great news of salvation for everyone to ourselves?
2.  What do you think about Mark Twain's statement?
3.  How does it make you feel when you hear of all the evil and misery that has resulted from the teaching of eternal damnation?
4.  How might we help lay to rest the myth of eternal damnation?
5.  Why do people resemble the gods they serve?
6.  What do you think about the fact that some of the most devoutly religious people have done so much evil, including crucifying Jesus?
7.  How will the world become a better place if we love our enemies?

# Lesson Thirteen

# SILENCE IS NOT GOLDEN

## A Handbook on Spreading the Wonderful News of Salvation for Everyone

If you want to tell others the good news of universal salvation but wonder how you can best do that, please read on. I will share with you how you might effectively share the news of salvation with others, what you can expect to happen when you do, and how you can utilize people's reactions (positive or negative) to help further the cause.

It is important to realize we are not on our own in our endeavor to carry out this great calling from God. We are privileged to be a part of God's plan of salvation. Through it all, God is with us. It is very helpful to spend much time in prayer, to seek God's guidance and inspiration, to be Christ-like in all situations, to be patient, loving, kind, forgiving, understanding, supportive, and Spirit-led. We also need to pray for others, that they may be receptive to all God has to offer them.

It is also very important that we who believe in universal salvation support each other. Others of like mind and spirit can help us maintain a positive attitude even if people do not always respond as favorably as we would like. Do not be discouraged if you do not already have Universalist friends. It is usually not difficult to find people for that kind of support group because some people already believe in universal salvation and many others are receptive to it. Besides, you will discover that often a very strong bond quickly develops between you and others who believe in salvation for everyone.

There are some churches that officially endorse universal salvation, and some in which the minister or others promote it even though it is contrary to their church's official doctrine, but they are not easy to find. Do not let that discourage you. You can effectively promote universalism in and through churches where there is overall receptivity to the teaching, as well as with churches where there is opposition to universalism among the members. You also can promote it very effectively outside of the Church.

## Responses You Can Expect

Unchurched people are usually very receptive to the belief that God will eventually succeed in saving everyone. Often the reason they are unchurched is because they have been driven from the Church by the teaching of a judgmental God. So they almost always receive universalism as wonderful, liberating good news.

Many people who attend church are also quite receptive to universal salvation. In contrast to the unchurched, however, church members' responses fall along the entire spectrum from enthusiastically positive to extremely negative. Their responses make life very interesting.

Some people already staunchly believe that God will eventually save everyone, and are well versed in the theological reasons why it is so. Others, who are not as confident, believe in universalism but they may not know that the belief is theologically well founded. They are among those who may have arrived at the conclusion more out of instinct than theological training. Most people who believe in universalism do not know that there are many others who believe the same way. Because of that, when you share your views with them, they will often embrace you with open arms out of appreciation that someone has finally expressed what they believe. They will be delighted to find in you a kindred spirit.

Many people have never heard of the concept of universal salvation and have not thought of it as a possibility. Not knowing better, they are ones who have been carrying with them the burden of the perception of a wrathful, judgmental God. Upon being told in a way that is convincing enough to overcome perhaps life-long negative indoctrination regarding God, they receive the news of salvation for everyone as a breath of fresh air. Upon realizing that God is really loving, forgiving and saving of everyone, they begin to celebrate the good news. They are delighted to be liberated.

Some people receive the news of universal salvation in a thoughtful way. They find it interesting, but it is a new idea to them and they are not convinced of its truth. While they are not ready to embrace universalism, they support your right to believe it. Others disagree with the idea that God will eventually save everyone. They believe that those who hold to the belief are wrong, but they tolerate you as one who does believe it, and perhaps will agree to disagree. A few people (primarily fundamentalist Christians) take very strong exception to the teaching of universalism, and tell you how wrong they think you are.

The first thing we need to affirm regarding the various responses to universal salvation is that each person is where he or she needs to be at that time on their spiritual journey. Where they are is all right with God and should be with us as well.

It is also good to keep in mind that the teaching of universalism is a new idea to most people. It is not realistic to expect everyone to embrace it immediately because they often have deeply ingrained and long-standing beliefs to the contrary. With some time and further thought, however, many of the ones who initially respond with skepticism and negativity will eventually come to believe in universal salvation.

## Utilizing Opposition

It is extremely helpful to realize that the small numbers of people who respond most negatively are in reality your co-workers in spreading the good news of salvation for everyone. Of course, they do not realize they are helping you through their criticism of you. Also, because of the pain they can sometimes inflict upon you, it may take considerable time and graciousness on your part before you are able to realize and fully appreciate how helpful they are to the cause of spreading universalism.

The reason the critics are so helpful is because they often tell others about your beliefs and how misguided they think you are. That creates enough of a stir that an ever-increasing number of people begin to talk about it. As the word spreads through the controversy, other people wonder what the fuss is all about. That motivates them to find out more about universalism. Upon learning about universal salvation and why it is so important, the majority of those people are very receptive to it. Some of the new adherents to universalism become strong proponents of the teaching, and proceed to freely tell others about it. That generates more controversy, which results in further spreading the good news of salvation for everyone, and so on.

Let us not forget that, while it is much more pleasant and enjoyable to speak of universal salvation to those who happily receive it, it is often through controversy that the news of universalism is most effectively spread. The natural tendency for most of us is to shy away from controversy and to avoid negative responses from others if at all possible. The key thing we need to remember in this regard is that if we timidly try to avoid unpleasant reactions from others, we will probably end up not saying anything to anyone about universal salvation, and those who promote doom and gloom will continue to prevail. But if we are courageous enough to not only endure some negative reactions from a few people, but also utilize it, we can make a powerful difference in the lives of countless people who yearn for good news.

I am well aware that it is especially risky for clergy to promote the teaching of universal salvation. Most ministers serve churches in denominations that officially adhere to the teaching of everlasting punishment in hell for the unsaved. If ministers of those churches promote universalism, they run the risk of encountering significant opposition from a few of their church members.

In my contacts with other ministers, I have found that a major percentage of them believe in universal salvation but most of them never teach it or even openly admit it to their parishioners. They are afraid of losing their jobs. I can understand that. I did the same thing for many years. I will always remember the first sermon I preached on the subject of universalism. I naively thought everyone would think it was wonderful and exciting good news, and respond favorably. Most people did, but a few very negative outspoken ones did not. I did not have the courage to speak of it again for years.

Having been intimidated into silence, while knowing I should speak up, kept eating at me over time, and I have finally gotten to the place where I can no longer keep quiet. There is too much at stake to bow to intimidation. It is a small, although loud and intimidating, minority of people who have in the past prevented the spread of universalism. The rest of us have been intimidated into letting them do it. No more!

The good news is that there is no reason for us to be intimidated. The bark of those in opposition is much worse than their bite. Besides, they are a small minority. Most people respond favorably, so we can feel free to stand up and be counted, to faithfully spread the wonderful news about God's unconditional love, unlimited power, undying grace, unmerited favor; God's salvation for everyone.

## Hopefulness Through Faithful Leadership

It saddens me to recognize that, because of the risk to them, we probably cannot rely on the clergy to lead in this great movement. If we are going to be successful within the churches in our endeavor to spread the wonderful news of salvation for everyone, lay members will probably have to take the primary responsibility to carry the banner. They have a great advantage over the clergy in that they do not run the risk of getting fired. They, just as the clergy, however, are sometimes subjected to the same negative reactions from those who oppose the teaching of universalism. I encourage those of you who are laity to muster the necessary courage and faithfulness to overcome that opposition. If you take the lead and pave the way, many of your ministers will eventually realize it is safe, and will openly join you in the cause.

I want you to know that, while you may lose a few church members if you proclaim the good news of salvation for everyone, there will be many, many others who will come into the church specifically because of your stand.

It appears to me that perhaps the greatest hope for spreading the news of universal salvation could take place outside of the Church, as a grass-roots movement. There is virtually no opposition to the teaching among the unchurched. People outside the Church have no turf to defend. There is no worry of offending other church members. They also do not have to overcome the co-dependence that often exists in churches.

I realize it may seem perplexing to many people that those who do not attend church could lead a spiritual movement. But let us give that some more thought. While many people find church participation to be extremely helpful to them on their spiritual journey, surely we can all agree that it is not necessary to go to church in order to be a Christian or to be spiritually mature. I have met many unchurched people who have the Spirit of Christ in them and are very advanced spiritually. They are well qualified to lead in the cause of universalism.

In order to experience the greatest possible success in our efforts to spread the news of salvation for everyone through Christ, all of us who believe in it will need to do our part; clergy and lay church members, as well as those who are outside the Church.

## The Blessing of Persecution

Let us take Matthew 5:11-12 as our Scriptural theme; "Blessed are you when people revile you and persecute you and utter all kinds of evil against you falsely on my account. Rejoice and be glad, for your reward is great in heaven, for in the same way they persecuted the prophets who were before you." Not only does the experience of persecution put us in very good company (with the prophets and Jesus), but also it is precisely through persecution and controversy that the belief in universalism is spread.

The opponents of the teaching that Christ has provided salvation for everyone cannot squash the movement today like they did in the sixth century. We enjoy much greater freedom (of religion, press, etc.), and have the benefits of the mass media and instant communications. The Church does not exercise total control anymore. The threat of excommunication falls on deaf ears.

Christianity has always flourished in the midst of adversity. It is well known that such was the case during the first several decades following the time of Christ. The same principle applies to spreading the news of universal salvation. In the late eighteenth and early nineteenth century in the United States, the Universalist movement encountered significant opposition but rose to its greatest strength in modern times. In spite of persecution, or because of it, the Universalists grew rapidly in numbers, reaching several hundred thousand adherents in the United States by 1850.

Sadly, the organized Universalist movement declined substantially during the twentieth century. But the cause is not lost. It is a new day and God's Spirit is moving in our midst. People are spiritually hungry for good news. A growing number of people are coming to believe in universal salvation and to freely share it with others.

If we follow the example of the early Universalists in boldly and broadly proclaiming the good news of salvation for everyone, and are willing to endure some opposition, the Universalist cause will again grow to a mighty movement. This will take place, not only in spite of persecution, but also because of it. We will restore the belief to prominence, as it was during the first centuries of the Christian Church.

And we will rejoice and be glad.

STUDY/DISCUSSION QUESTIONS:
1. How much opposition are you willing to endure in order to spread the great news of salvation for everyone?
2. What do you think about those who respond most negatively having the effect of being our co-workers in promoting universalism?
3. What can you do to encourage clergy to join the cause?
4. Of those you know who do not go to church, might they be unchurched because of the teaching of eternal damnation?
5. What do you think about the idea that, at any given time, people are where they need to be on their spiritual journey?
6. Do you know people outside the church who are more advanced spiritually than many who go to church?

# NOTES

**LESSON TWO:** DARE TO POSSESS THE TRUTH: What Does the Bible Say Regarding Universal Salvation?

1. Robert Young, *Analytical Concordance to the Bible* (Grand Rapids: William B. Eerdman's Publishing Company, 1970), p. 308.
2. Ibid., pp. 308, 310.
3. *The Interpreter's Bible: A Commentary in Twelve Volumes*, Vol. 11 (Nashville: Abingdon Press, 1955), p. 51.

**LESSON THREE:** SEEING THE BIGGER PICTURE: General Biblical Themes

1. Raymond A. Moody Jr., *Life After Life* (New York: Bantam Books, 1975), p. 59.
2. Raymond A. Moody Jr., *Reflections on Life After Life* (New York: Bantam Books, 1977), p. 32.

**LESSON FOUR:** AMAZING GRACE: Implications of Universal Salvation Versus Eternal Damnation

1. L. A. King, "Hell, the Painful Refuge", *Eternity Magazine*, January 1979, p. 29.

**LESSON FIVE:** I WANT TO DO IT MYSELF: Do We Have Free Will?

1. Robert Short, *Something To Believe In* (New York: Harper & Row Publishers, 1978), p. 250.
2. Ibid., p. 54.
3. Ibid.

4. *The Works of John Wesley*, Vol. 2, Sermons 34-70, Ed. Albert C. Outler, (Nashville: Abingdon Press, 1985), p. 490.

**LESSON SIX:** LAYING A SOLID FOUNDATION: What God Is Like

1. L. Robert Keck, *Sacred Eyes* (Boulder: Synergy Associates, Inc., 1992), p. 49.

**LESSON SEVEN:** FREE AT LAST: From Hell to Heaven-- How it is Accomplished

1. Walter Wink, *Engaging the Powers* (Minneapolis: Fortress Press, 1992), p. 268.

**LESSON EIGHT:** GOING BEYOND WISHFUL THINKING: The Power of Unconditional Love

1. Melody Beattie, *The Language of Letting Go* (Center City, MN: Hazelden Foundation, 1990), p. 95.

**LESSON NINE:** FORGIVENESS IS ONLY THE BEGINNING: Growing into God's Likeness

1. M. Scott Peck, *Further Along The Road Less Traveled* (New York: Simon & Schuster, 1993), pp. 120-131.

**LESSON ELEVEN:** THE ANCIENTS HAVE STOLEN OUR BEST IDEAS: The History of Universalism

1. *The Columbian Congress of the Universalist Church* (Boston: Universalist Publishing House, 1883), p. 158.
2. Ibid., p. 170.
3. Origen, *On First Principals*, Trans. G. W. Butterworth (New York: Harper & Row, Publishers, 1966), p. 146.

4. John Wesley Hanson, *Aion—Aionios: the Greek Word Translated Everlasting—Eternal, in the Holy Bible, Shown to Denote Limited Duration* (Chicago: Northwestern Universalist Publishing House, 1876), p. 71. Also: Columbian Congress, p. 158.
5. Ibid., pp. 147-148.
6. Ibid., p. 147.
7. Ibid., p. 159.
8. Brian E. Daley, *The Hope of the Early Church: A Handbook of Patristic Eschatology* (Cambridge: Cambridge University Press, 1991), p. 85.
9. Ibid., p. 97.
10. Williston Walker, *A History of the Christian Church* (New York: Charles Scribner's Sons, 1970), pp. 160-162.
11. *The Fathers of the Church, Vol. 24, Saint Augustine, The City of God*, Trans. Gerald G. Walsh and Daniel J. Donan (Washington, D. C.: The Catholic University of America Press, 1954), pp. 378-379.
12. Daley., p. 189.; Also Hanson, p. 74.
13. Ibid., pp. 188, 189, 190.
14. Columbian Congress, p. 174.
15. *The Works of John Wesley*, Vol. 2, pp. 400, 410, 411.
16. *Colliers Encyclopedia*, Vol. 22 (Crowell-Collier Educational Corporation, 1969), p. 741.
17. Ibid.
18. Russell E. Miller, *The Larger Hope: The First Century of the Universalist Church in America, 1770-1870* (Boston: Unitarian Universalist Association, 1979), pp. 11-12.
19. Ibid., pp. 13-33.
20. Ibid., p. 21.
21. Ernest Cassara, *Hosea Ballou; The Challenge to Orthodoxy* (Boston: Universalist Historical Society and Beacon Press, 1961), pp. 151, 167.
22. *The Unitarian Universalist Pocket Guide*, Ed. William F. Schulz (Boston: Skinner House Books, 1993), p. 89.
23. Dietrich Bonhoeffer, *Ethics*, Ed. Eberhard Bethge (New York: The Macmillan Company, 1945), pp. 70-71.

24. Karl Barth, *Church Dogmatics*, Vol. 2, Part 2, (Edinburgh: T. & T. Clark, 1957), p. 306.
25. Paul Tillich, *The Eternal Now* (New York: Charles Scribner's Sons, 1963), p. 121.

**LESSON TWELVE:** MAKING MOUNTAINS OUT OF MOUNTAINS: The Significance of This Issue

1. Mark Twain, *The Mysterious Stranger* (New York: Harper & Brothers Publishers, 1916), pp. 150-151.
2. Short, p. 88.
3. Anton Szander LaVey, *The Satanic Bible* (New York: Avon Books, 1969), p. 86.
4. Ibid., p. 54.
5. Short, p. 253.
6. John Godsey, Ed., *Karl Barth's Table Talk* (Richmond: John Knox Press, 1962), p. 87.

Destined for Salvation Ministries is affiliated with Universalist Christians Association Inc., an interdenominational non-profit organization.

The mission of the Universalist Christians Association Inc. is to assist in spreading the Good News brought to us by Jesus Christ: The Good News that God's love is so complete and so powerful that all will eventually be brought to salvation, redemption and eternal life. To this end, the purposes of the Universalist Christians Association Inc. are:

1. To explore, nurture and promote Universalist Christianity within and across Christian communities.
2. To provide support and fellowship for individual Universalist Christians as they bear witness to their faith.
3. To educate the general public as to the history and nature of Universalist Christianity.

To invite Rev. Fristad to speak to your church or group, or order copies of this book ($5.95; ten or more, $5.45), or his other book ($11.95; ten or more, $10.95), contact Destined For Salvation Ministries: 1403 W. 2$^{nd}$ St. N., Newton, Iowa 50208, 641-787-9040, www.universalistchristians.org.